INTRODUCTION

About Freekeh and Supergrains

People refer to certain grains as 'the new supergrain' or 'the latest supergrain', which is quite amusing considering that ancient grains mean exactly that – ancient!

Many grains have been around for thousands of years and were, in fact, one of the only sources of food along with plants that was relatively obtainable. The impact that healthy food can have on our well-being is without doubt and the purer the product, the better it is for us. Supergrains are undoubtedly packed full of beneficial nutrients and should not be disregarded as part of our regular dietary intake. Some supergrains are relatively household words these days, but there are others that are beginning to emerge with meteoric popularity, one of which is **freekeh** or **freekah**, **frikeh** and **farik** as it can be called, along with a few lesser known names.

This book is your 'freekeh bible' – every recipe is based on the use of this wonderful grain in your recipes, with surprising uses for it. You can more or less substitute freekeh for any other grain that you would normally use, adapting the recommended way of cooking and preparing it. Simple to use, tasty to eat, there is no reason why you could not become a freekeh fan.

In this day and age, time is important as we all lead such busy lives, so the bulk of the recipes in this book are made using **'cracked freekeh'** ie. freekeh that has already been refined via a cooking process and needs very little preparation time. **Wholegrain freekeh** can of course be used in all the recipes, but does add double or treble the time to the preparation of a dish. The benefits of using the pure wholegrain freekeh as opposed to cracked freekeh is the amount of nutrients it contains far outstrips the length of time taken in preparation. Refined grains have the bran and germ removed, which leaves simply the endosperm which has less nutrients than the rest of the grain, but is still worthwhile as part of your regular diet.

The move towards supergrains is undoubtedly for their versatility as well as their health benefits, or simply a lifestyle choice such as veganism or vegetarianism. They are certainly tastier as well, with a much deeper flavour and texture than highly refined grains.

So try freekeh with all of its benefits and make a difference to your life.

What is Freekeh?

Freekeh is under-ripe (green) wheat that is picked before maturity, sundried and then roasted over straw and chaff – the unique 'smoky and earthy' flavour is a result of its preparation. The final 'rubbing' process of the grain has a lot to do with its texture, flavour and unique colour. The name 'freekeh' actually means 'to rub' in Arabic. Because the grains are harvested young, they retain the maximum nutritional value which also impacts on the wonderful flavour of the grain. Freekeh is somewhat known as the 'smoky cousin of bulgur wheat' which is an apt description although it is certainly nuttier than its relative.

History of Freekeh

Whilst we are aware that freekeh dates back thousands of years and can be traced back to ancient Egypt, Lebanon, Jordan and Syria, there is a wonderful story of how it was discovered.

The rather fabulistic tale accredits one of the Eastern Mediterranean nations of discovering freekeh more by the threat of war, rather than scientific study! In 2300 BC as the tale goes, the nation was under threat of attack on one of their cities, so frightened about losing their young crop, the townsfolk picked the green heads off the wheat and stored them en masse. There was no respite from the threat and whilst in the throes of battle, the storehouse was set fire to and the wheat was destroyed (or so they thought!). On viewing the devastation of the crop, an aspiring equivalent of a modern day Heston Blumenthal decided to rub the wheat heads and taste them, and found them to be delicious! With no other explanations as to how freekeh originated, we are quite happy to stick with that one!

Whilst this story revolves around four nations, freekeh is popular throughout the Middle East and has been for thousands of years and can be traced to other countries such as Egypt, Iraq, North Africa, Turkey and parts of Greece and the Islands. An early 13th Century cook book from Iraq mentions a dish called *'farikiyya'* which with the addition of milk and honey was believed to be beneficial to women giving birth!

Whatever story you can find about freekeh and its origins, the facts still remain in terms of its beneficial properties.

Freekeh Health and Nutrition

In depth modern research has discovered many facts about freekeh and its beneficial properties. The table below shows that the nutritional components overall are better for you in comparison to other grains

Based on One Serving of 42 grams*

	Quinoa	Brown Rice	Farro	Freekeh	
Calories	155	170	170	150	✓
Total Fat	1.3g	2g	1g	1.5g	✓
Total Carbs	30g	38g	35g	30g	✓
Dietary Fibre	3g	2g	5g	6g	✓
Protein	5.5g	4g	7g	6g	✓
Calcium	0mg	0mg	2mg	25mg	✓
Iron	2%	2%	1%	2.2mg	✓

*Information kindly supplied by University of Adelaide, Australia, University of Surrey, United Kingdom, CSIRO, Australia, and AGAL Australia, as well as medical publications.

Table of Contents

INTRODUCTION 3

BREAKFAST AND MORNING COFFEE TIME 16
   Freekeh Carrot, Coconut and Goji Berry Muffins 17
   Freekeh 'Feelgood' Flapjacks 20
   Freekeh Granola Bars 23
   Fruit and Nut Freekeh Cookies 26
   Fruity Freekeh Porridge 29
   Smoked Salmon and Scrambled Eggs with
      Freekeh Potato Cakes 31
   Tropical Scented Freekeh Fruit Salad 34

CAKES AND LOAVES 36
   Freekeh Coffee and Walnut Cake 37
   Spiced Pumpkin and Freekeh Loaf 40

DESSERTS AND SNACKS 44
   Apricot Freekeh Dessert 45
   Banana Freekeh Kisses 47
   Freekeh Blackberry and Apple Crumble 49
   Freekeh Pizza Margharita for the Kids! 52
   Freekeh with Honey Roasted Figs and Ricotta 54
   Wholesome Freekeh Vegetable Stew 57

DINNERS 60
   Beef Stroganoff with Minted Pea Freekeh 61
   Chilli Con Carne with Freekeh 64
   Easy Freekeh Lamb Biryani 67
   Freekeh Mushroom and Herb Pilaff 70
   Freekeh Sausage and Chips for Little Ones! 73
   Freekeh Shrimp Gumbo 76

Freekeh Vegetable Bake 79
Herb Crusted Salmon with Spinach Freekeh 82
Maple Roasted Chicken with Freekeh Stuffing 85
Marvellous Freekeh Meatloaf 88
Mediterranean Freekeh Stuffed Peppers 91
Mexican Beef and Freekeh Pizza 94
Roasted Root Vegetables with Freekeh 97
Roasted Vegetable Freekeh Soup 100
Roasted Balsamic Beets with Freekeh and Yoghurt 103
Slow Cooked Pork and Lentil Casserole with
    Apple and Freekeh 106
Spicy Freekeh Veggie Burgers 109
Succulent Beef Freekeh Olives 112
Sweet and Sour Chicken with Freekeh 115
Tofu and Freekeh Vegetable Stir Fry 118
Traditional Tabbouleh 121
Turkey Stuffed "Beefsteak" Tomatoes 123
Turkey Freekeh Meatball and Pineapple Curry 126

SALADS 129
A Taste of the Islands Freekeh Salad 130
Avocado Freekeh Salad with Sumac 133
Freekeh Feta Greek Salad 136
Simple Freekeh Buffet Salad 138
Tuna Freekeh Provencale 141
Zingy Thai Chicken and Mango Freekeh Salad 143

SNACKS 146
Freekeh Chocolate Biscuit Cakes 147
Freekeh Meatless Meatballs (Felafels) 149
Freekeh Sausage and Red Pepper Rolls 152
Rustic Freekeh Bruschettas 155
Zucchini and Freekeh Fritters 157
California Sushi Roll with Pickled Ginger 160

INDEX 163

Benefits – why is freekeh so healthy?

- Loaded with fibre, excellent for regularity of bowel movements, aids in laxation, IBS and reduces the risk of diverticulitis
- Low carbohydrates – resistant starch which behaves like fibre and keeps you full
- Plenty of protein, more than most grains due to the preparation process
- Low fat content, of which majority is 'healthy fat' for heart and system
- Good probiotics, which rebalance the intestinal system
- Low Glycaemic Index – excellent insulin response, great for diabetics
- Weight Loss/Reduced Risk of Obesity – quick and easy transition through the body

- Promotes eye health, due to the presence of eye protective antioxidants such as lutein and zeaxanthin. Aids in the prevention of macular degeneration.
- Perfect substitute for rice and other grains and suitable for **vegans** and **vegetarians.**

There are a multitude of other health benefits including high calcium and high iron – particularly useful for females prone to brittle bone disease and also pregnant women with an iron deficiency respectively. Please remember that you should consult your medical practitioner before any changes in diet if you have any particular medical problems.

A Word about Gluten…

It is important to remember that freekeh is a wheat based product, and as such contains levels of gluten, which is not suitable for people with wheat allergies. Whilst the allergens in gluten are reduced during cooking, it is probably best to avoid it.

Cooking with Freekeh

Freekeh is very simple to cook with and can take on a variety of flavours during cooking or matches well once cooked. Its flavour characteristics such as its nutty and herbaceous taste pair well with other robust herbs and spices such as mint, rosemary, coriander, cumin and paprika, as well as other stronger Middle Eastern spices such as Ras-al-Hanout, Sumac and sweeter spices such as nutmeg and cinnamon. Salads, pilaffs, stews, soups, meat, vegetables and most fish will benefit from the accompaniment of freekeh. Almost anywhere you use rice, you can replace it with freekeh. You are also able to pair it with fruit in breakfasts and desserts, along with cakes and breads. As stated before, freekeh is a very versatile grain.

Cooking freekeh couldn't be simpler, either on the oven top or using a rice cooker.

As a guideline:

Oven Top -

Wholegrain Freekeh

- 7oz/200g
- 55-60fl.oz/1½-2 litres water
- 45-50 minutes cook time.
- Yield – 14oz/400g cooked freekeh.
- Cook on gentle boil; if water evaporates add a little more until freekeh is fully cooked and swollen.

Cracked Freekeh

- 7oz/200g
- 11fl.oz/300ml

15-20 minutes cook time, more or less same yield. Bring to boil and leave on high simmer until water absorbed.

You can cook the freekeh in stock or bouillon or broth of any flavour, i.e. chicken, beef etc. if you are not a vegetarian or vegan.

Rice Cooker –

A little trickier, but as a general rule freekeh should cook at the same rate as brown rice. However in terms of grains/ratio of liquid, you may have to experiment a few times to get it to perfection.

Freekeh can also be cooked using slow cookers/crockpots and generally takes 6-8 hours along with the meat that you choose to cook. You can also cook freekeh using a pressure cooker, but this is not so easy and even following charts supplied with your pressure cooker, you may find the need to adjust liquid content and timings for wholegrains. You are also able to cook freekeh in the microwave, but again, experimentation is needed.

Our recipes involve cooking freekeh in the usual basic way, but please do use your imagination and try other methods until you find the perfect way for you to produce the results you want.

Remember, once the freekeh is cooked, drain off any remaining water if possible and dry the freekeh as best as you can. Freekeh also benefits from being rinsed to remove any 'scum' from the dish. It won't do you any harm, but certainly looks better if used in salads.

Recommendations

When cooking with freekeh, at first it will seem difficult to calculate exactly how much you need – we always end up with more than is needed, but this is actually a good thing as you can use freekeh in many 'leftover' recipes such as stir frys, fritters, soups and salads where you may normally have used rice, pasta, orzo or spelt. It is a substitute for any grain that you may be used to using.

Freekeh does expand whilst cooking but not as much as rice, and it is definitely tastier. Freekeh flour is also available, but is much harder to find and certainly not available from normal sources. You can try smaller Middle Eastern shops for both the grains and flour.

You can also freeze cooked freekeh in batches, so keep a stock of ziplock bags in your store cupboard. Freeze for one month, an ideal time. You will find that when eating freekeh dishes, you will not need as much cooked grain because as a starch, it keeps you feeling fuller for longer.

Try to keep your store cupboard well stocked with plenty of dried herbs and spices, jars of tomato puree or tinned tomatoes, and other useful items such as roasted peppers in oil, sundried tomatoes etc. – most foodstuffs can be used with freekeh, and having the ability to put your hand in your cupboard and pull out a tasty accompaniment will encourage you to create freekeh dishes in a matter of moments. Asian flavours are also delicious with freekeh, so a selection of pastes such as curry, wasabi, black bean and miso, along with soy sauce, sweet chilli sauce and oyster sauce can add depth of flavour to your dishes.

We frequently use fresh herbs in our recipes, as much for appearance as for the taste. Fresh herbs in a freekeh salad or pilaff are ultimately more appealing than dried. Mint, parsley, rosemary, coriander and oregano are some of the herbs we tend to use.

Good quality stock is also essential to bring your dishes to life and to get maximum flavour. If you are not in the habit of making your own, always buy the best that you can find in your local supermarket, it is invaluable to you.

Nuts and seeds have a long shelf life, and are very good for you unless you are allergy prone. Sesame seeds and Chia seeds (black and white) are our favourites for coating fish or chicken, and pine nuts, pistachios and almonds fare best with salads and pilaffs. One of our all-time favourites to use are fresh pomegranate seeds – so delicious with spiced lamb and great with salads. These juicy little balls of deep pinky red flesh and lovely nutty little seeds in the middle add an amazing dimension to any dish.

Keep plenty of pulses in your cupboard, such as canned lentils, kidney beans, flageolet beans, borlotti beans and chickpeas. These also provide a considerable amount of fibre, even in small quantities, and are a wholesome and warming food, particularly in cold and wet months. Most can also be used in salads, or as dips when crushed or liquidised.

Intro and Book Freekeh

There is no substitute for wonderful fresh vegetables, either of the Mediterranean type such as peppers and zucchini, or good leafy green vegetables such as cabbage, kale and spinach. The humble pea, either fresh or frozen is also full of nutrients and is quite adaptable, as are green beans and broad beans. Most frozen vegetables retain a considerable amount of their original vitamins, so don't discount them.

Root vegetables such as potatoes, sweet potatoes, parsnips, swede etc., are also good for you, but remember they carry quite a high carbohydrate level. Used in small quantities and roasted is a good way to go.

Whilst childrens' palates are much more mature these days and they are used to eating many more types of foods than some years ago, so we have included some child friendly recipes. Pizzas and cakes, bread and desserts, will certainly become favourites of theirs with the use of freekeh. Use some of the healthy recipes in their lunchboxes as well as enjoying some of them yourself.

Enjoy !

Other 'great grains'....

Whilst we genuinely believe that Freekeh is one of the best grains for health and nutrition, there are some other ancient grains that do a really good job of keeping you healthy and providing the nutrition that you need. You can substitute the freekeh in the majority of our recipes for any of these wonderful grains. Here is a list of the lesser used grains and their properties. Most of the ancient grains all have a nutty and sometimes earthy texture, so strong flavours are acceptable to use.

AMARANTH	Herby and 'grassy', slightly gelatinous when cooked. Good with sweet partners (chocolate, honey) but also with spices such as cinnamon, chilli and paprika
CHIA	A mild flavour, which pairs well with most savoury or sweet foods and is also good for 'coating'. Dried fruit, nuts and other seeds are also good partners, along with sprinkling on salads, smoothies and dressings.
KAMUT	Very buttery and nutty, goes well with similar flavoured foods that are slightly sweet and nutty, particularly any roasted vegetables, baked bread, or stuffings.
FARRO	Cracked farro has a nutty taste and chewy texture, frequently used in Italian foods using cured meats, herbs, parmesan, but can also be used in salads, risottos, soups and stews.
QUINOA	Probably the most well-known grain, extremely versatile with a soft but slightly bitter flavour and a nutty texture. Pairs well with Mediterranean or Middle Eastern recipes, and with herbs, and citrus flavours. Can be used in more or less any meal from salads to stews, porridge to pilaff. Quinoa flakes make a delicious porridge.

SPELT The uses of spelt are very similar to quinoa in their good match with Mediterranean foods, and including cheese and herbs. Also good for stuffings and breadmaking. Nutty and earthy in flavour.

TEFF The world's tiniest grain, but packed with nutrients. It varies in colour from a dark reddy-brown to ivory. The paler the grain, the milder the flavour, but overall a nutty taste and texture, likened to hazelnuts.

Breakfast AND Morning Coffee Time

Freekeh Carrot, Coconut and Goji Berry Muffins

May sound an unusual combination, but the end result is a lovely moist muffin, with a hint of spice and the nutty sweetness of the coconut. Goji berries are of course a superfood, so combined with the freekeh, you have a few tasty mouthfuls of goodness. There are a lot of ingredients for this recipe, but they really are worth that extra effort. The making of the muffins couldn't be simpler!

Serves: 16 medium sized muffins or 24 small muffins

Preparation Time: 5-10 minutes

Cook Time: 25-30 minutes

Ingredients:

- 7oz/200g of freekeh, cooked
- 13oz/370g wholemeal flour
- 3½oz/100g brown sugar
- 3tsp baking soda
- 1lb/450g carrots, grated
- 3oz/85g dried goji berries
- 5 eggs, beaten
- 3oz/85g dried coconut
- 1tsp cinnamon

- 1tsp ground mixed spice
- 8oz/225g applesauce
- 8fl.oz/240ml canola or vegetable oil
- 1tsp vanilla extract
- Juice and grated rind of 1 large orange
- 4oz/115g almonds, walnuts, or pecans if required, chopped or dried banana chips

Method:

Heat oven to 180°C/350°F/Gas mark 4

In a muffin tray, or on a flat baking sheet, place the correct size paper cake cups or silicone cake cups.

Mix all the dry ingredients together in one bowl. In a separate bowl, mix together all the wet ingredients. Add the wet ingredients to the dry, a little at a time, and mix thoroughly after each addition.

Fill each cake case up to approximately two-thirds full. If you are going to use nuts or banana chips, split the mixture into two, so that you have some muffins without nuts.

Bake in the oven for 30-35 minutes, or until a knife inserted into the middle of a muffin comes out clean. Remove from the oven to cool.

Nutritional Analysis	Per medium muffin (16th)
Energy	137kcal
Protein	6g
Carbohydrates	33g
of which sugars	11g
Total Fat	1g
of which saturates	1g
Fibre	5g
Sodium	22g

Freekeh 'Feelgood' Flapjacks

A treat at teatime or with a morning coffee, you will adore this version of flapjacks. With healthy oats and freekeh, some fruit and maple or agave syrup, these are a lovely slightly chewy delight.

Serves: 12 medium or 20 smaller pieces

Preparation Time: 10 minutes

Cook Time: 50 minutes

Ingredients:

- 2oz/55g butter, plus a little for greasing
- 3tbsp maple or agave syrup, or raw honey

- 2tbsp peanut butter (smooth is better, but you can use chunky)
- 2 ripe bananas, mashed
- 1 apple, peeled and grated, some moisture removed
- 5oz/140g rolled oats
- 5oz/140g freekeh
- Hot water

Method:

Heat oven to 160°C/325°F/Gas Mark 3.

Grease and line an 8in/20cm square tin with parchment paper.

In a small pan, melt the butter, peanut butter and maple syrup, stirring together. Add the bananas and apple, followed by the hot water. Stir to combine.

In a separate bowl, mix the oats and freekeh together. Add the wet ingredients and stir thoroughly to combine. Pour into the prepared cake tin and smooth over the surface.

Bake for 50 minutes until lovely and golden on the top and set. Leave to cool, then cut into bars or squares (smaller pieces are advisable as it is quite rich).

Store in an airtight container in the fridge. The treats will keep up to 4 days if left in the fridge.

Nutritional Analysis	Per Portion
Energy	162kl (small piece)
Protein	6g
Carbohydrates	23g
of which sugars	7g
Total Fat	8g
of which saturates	3g
Fibre	10g
Sodium	0.1g

Freekeh Granola Bars

These are great bars for a quick breakfast, or a snack in the car if you haven't had time to sit down and eat. Also a useful and healthy snack in lunchboxes and for the children. Make up batches and keep in airtight containers, they will last for probably up to two weeks. You can vary the mix of seeds, nuts and dried fruit according to your own taste.

Serves: 12 bars

Preparation Time: 15 minutes

Cook Time: 30 minutes

Ingredients:

- 3½oz/100g butter
- 3½oz/100g freekeh, cooked
- 3½oz/100g rolled oats
- 2oz/55g sunflower seeds
- 2oz/55g sesame seeds
- 2oz/55g chopped walnuts or almonds if you prefer
- 3tbsp raw honey
- 3½oz/100g light muscovado sugar
- 1tsp ground cinnamon
- 3½oz/100g mixed dried berries, such as blueberries, cranberries or cherries

Method:

Heat oven to 160°C/325°F/Gas mark 3

Butter and line a 7 x 10inch/18 x 25cm tin with parchment paper.

In a baking tray, lightly toast the oats, seeds and nuts for 5-10 minutes.

Meanwhile, melt the butter, honey and sugar in a pan over a gentle heat, stirring well to prevent burning. Add the freekeh, oat mix, dried fruit and cinnamon. Mix well so that everything is coated.

Tip into the lined tin, press down lightly and bake for 30 minutes. Leave to cool and cut into bars (12 is a good number).

Nutritional Analysis	Per Portion
Energy	294kl
Protein	6g
Carbohydrates	30g
Total Fat	17g
of which saturates	6g
Fibre	3g
Sodium	0.14g

Fruit and Nut Freekeh Cookies

Nothing like being able to eat cookies that you know are healthy for you! Using freekeh and rolled oats is a great way to go without having a guilt trip! These cookies are lovely with your morning coffee or great in the children's lunchboxes.

Serves: 24 small or 16 larger cookies

Preparation Time: 10 minutes

Cook Time: 20-25 minutes depending on consistency required

Ingredients:

- 8oz/225g cooked freekeh
- 4½oz/135g cups rolled oats
- 1½oz/40g chopped hazelnuts
- 1½oz/40g mixed dried fruit (sultanas, raisins etc)
- 1½oz/40g dried cranberries
- 1½oz/40g dried apricots, chopped
- 2oz/55g cup brown sugar
- 6oz/170g raw honey
- 1½tbsp vegetable oil or canola oil
- 1tsp vanilla extract
- 2 large eggs, plus one egg white, lightly beaten

Method:

Heat oven to 325°C/160°F/Gas mark 3.

Mix together the cooked freekeh, rolled oats, nut, dried fruit, apricots, cranberries and sugar.

Beat the honey, oil and vanilla extract into the egg mix. Add the wet mix to the dry and combine thoroughly. The mixture should be of 'dropping consistency'. If a little dry, add a few drops of water. If a little wet, add some more oats or wholemeal flour.

Line a baking sheet with parchment paper and 'drop' the mixture on to it, leaving enough space between each drop so that the cookies don't stick together. For 36 cookies use 1 heaped tablespoon, for 24 cookies, use 2 level tablespoons for the desired size.

Flatten each drop slightly, but not too much, as these cookies look so much nicer when they are 'rustic'.

Bake for 15-20 minutes for 'chewy' cookies, or 20-25 minutes for crispier ones.

Enjoy with your morning coffee!

Nutritional Analysis	Per portion, large cookie
Energy	191kcal
Protein	5g
Carbohydrates	31g
of which sugars	17g
Total Fat	5g
of which saturates	1g
Fibre	3g
Sodium	.01g

Fruity Freekeh Porridge

As a child, porridge was fed to us as a 'warm winter lining' to protect against the cold on our way to school. It was never something particularly enjoyable and always tasted fairly bland. It is now enjoying a resurgence, especially using different grains and a rainbow array of dried or fresh fruits as toppings.

Serves: 4

Preparation Time: 5 minutes

Cook Time: 15 - 20 minutes

Ingredients:

- 9oz/250g freekeh
- Water
- 125ml/4fl.oz almond milk
- ½tsp salt
- 1tsp cinnamon
- 1tbsp maple syrup or raw honey
- 3oz/85g dried apricots, chopped
- 3oz/85g fresh blueberries or raspberries
- 3oz/85g pistachios, chopped

Method:

Cook the freekeh for 15 minutes in the required amount of water and the salt. Drain, put back in the pan with the almond milk, cinnamon and maple syrup and bring up to warm again, stirring to mix through. Add the dried apricots and continue to simmer for 5 minutes. In the meantime, toast the pistachios in a dry pan.

Remove the porridge from the heat and serve in bowls topped with the fresh blueberries and pistachios. You can also add sultanas or raisins if desired.

Nutritional Analysis	Per portion
Energy	363kcal
Protein	16g
Carbohydrates	62g
of which sugars	8g
Total Fat	22g
of which saturates	3g
Fibre	9g
Sodium	.1g

Smoked Salmon and Scrambled Eggs with Freekeh Potato Cakes

A breakfast or brunch to spoil you or your guests! The freekeh potato cakes can be a little tricky, so give yourself time in advance (even make the day before). They can be part fried and then frozen for future use, or left in the fridge to use the next day.

Serves: 4 (8 medium sized cakes)

Preparation Time: 25 minutes (less if you have left over mashed potato)

Cook Time: 5 minutes each side to fry, or 20 minutes in the oven

Ingredients:

For the cakes

- 5oz/140g leftover mashed potato, or two large potatoes cooked and mashed
- 5oz/140g freekeh, cooked
- Seasoning to taste (plenty of black pepper)
- A little flour to coat the cakes
- 1 small onion, grated (optional)
- 1tbsp vegetable oil for frying

For the scrambled eggs

- 5 large eggs
- 2tbsp single cream
- Seasoning to taste
- A little butter for scrambling
- 4/5oz-115/140g smoked salmon, cut into thin strips
- A few chopped chives to garnish

Method:

Heat oven to 180°C/350°F/Gas mark 4

In a medium sized bowl, mix together the potato, freekeh and seasoning. Form into 8 cakes/patties and coat in the flour. Heat oil in a frying pan and cook the cakes on each side for 3 minutes.

Place on an oiled baking tray and pop into the oven. Whilst the cakes are cooking, beat the eggs and cream, add the seasoning. Flip the cakes over after about 5 minutes.

Heat the butter in a pan until foaming, and pour in the egg mixture. Lightly scramble the eggs until just soft and no liquid can be seen.

Remove the cakes from the oven and place 2 on each plate, top with the eggs and drape the smoked salmon strips over the top. Add a scattering of chopped chives.

Serve with a little watercress and cherry tomatoes.

Nutritional Analysis	Per Portion
Energy	441kcal
Protein	26g
Carbohydrates	44g
of which sugars	3g
Total Fat	20g
of which saturates	12g
Fibre	5g
Sodium	.8g

Tropical Scented Freekeh Fruit Salad

The best of tropical soft fruits can be used in this recipe – mangoes, papayas, melons, pineapple and berries, the choice is up to you. With the addition of sweet scented basil and the zing of lime, you could be anywhere in the world.

If you enjoy this fruit salad, try using chopped mint the next time for a different experience. You can save time by cooking the freekeh the night before and leaving in the fridge.

Serves: 4

Preparation Time: 15-20 minutes

Cook Time: 20 minutes (for the freekeh)

Ingredients:

- 5oz/140g cooked freekeh
- 4oz/115g fresh pineapple, chopped
- 1 large mango, peeled, stone removed and chopped
- 4oz/115g fresh strawberries, hulled and quartered

- 6-8 fresh basil leaves, roughly shredded or torn
- Juice and zest of one lime
- 1tbsp agave nectar (or raw honey)
- 4tbsp 0% fat Greek Yoghurt (if desired)

Method:

Place the cooked freekeh in a large bowl. Stir in the agave nectar and add the lime juice and zest. Mix thoroughly.

Mix the fruit together in a separate bowl with the shredded basil.

Divide between 4 bowls, top with the fruit and a spoonful of yoghurt, or serve the yoghurt to the side.

Nutritional Analysis	Per portion
Energy	158kcal
Protein	9g
Carbohydrates	30g
of which sugars	11g
Total Fat	>1g
of which saturates	>1g
Fibre	5.75
Sodium	.01g

CAKES AND LOAVES

Freekeh Coffee and Walnut Cake

Probably the most indulgent recipe in this book! But you have to treat yourself sometimes, and keep in mind that freekeh is doing you good – as long as you don't eat the whole cake alone! We have added carrot to this recipe to keep the cake as moist as possible, and the freekeh has been 'milled' down in a food processor to give it a less grainy texture. All in all, great result!

Serves: 8

Preparation Time: 20 minutes

Cook Time: 50-60 minutes

Ingredients:

- 7oz/200g freekeh, blitzed in food processor for about 1 minute
- 5oz/140g carrots, grated
- 4oz/115g vegetable oil
- 3 eggs
- 6oz/170g sugar (raw sugar is better)
- 7oz/200g plain flour or wholemeal if you prefer
- 5oz/140g walnuts, chopped
- 1tsp baking powder
- 1tsp baking soda
- 2tbsp milk
- ½tbsp mixed spice, or more if you prefer a stronger, spicier taste
- 2tsps coffee essence

For the icing

- 1oz/30g icing sugar
- 3½oz/100g unsalted butter, softened
- 1tsp coffee essence
- Handful walnuts, chopped

Method:

Heat oven to 180°C/350°/Gas mark 4

Mix the carrots and freekeh together. Beat the eggs and add to the mixture.

Add all the remaining ingredients and combine thoroughly to remove any lumps, so that the batter is smooth as possible.

Pour into a lined loose bottomed cake tin (we used a 9 inch/23 cm tin) and bake in the oven for 50-60 minutes. Test the cake after 50 minutes by inserting skewer into the centre. It should come out clean – if not, cook for a further 5-10 minutes.

In the meantime, mix together your icing ingredients to a smooth paste.

Remove the cake from the oven, and leave to cool for 5-10 minutes in the tin. When cool enough to handle, turn out the cake onto a wire rack. Leave until totally cool.

Smooth over your icing, and scatter over the walnuts.

Nutritional Analysis	Per Portion
Energy	600kcal
Protein	11g
Carbohydrates	55g
of which sugars	37g
Total Fat	33g
of which saturates	16g
Fibre	4g
Sodium	.14g

Spiced Pumpkin and Freekeh Loaf

The weather is horrible – cold, windy and rainy. Maybe you have been walking the dog, or purely taking the children out for some fresh air and you need something to warm you up. This bread is delicious particularly when served warm with a bowl of chilli con carne or a casserole.

We have used a loaf tin to make this bread, but you can make it in a square dish, 20 x 20cm/8 x 8in. The lovely thing about making it in a loaf tin is that you get the rise as you would do in a nice crusty loaf of bread, and you can actually use it for sandwiches! It has a great texture and is a little less sweet than the traditional cornbread, particularly if you add a few unusual ingredients such as the onion or mustard seeds, or even some finely diced mild chilli, or sunflower/pumpkin seeds. It is quite unusual, and will be a great hit with the family or with guests. Sugar and spice and all things nice!!

Serves: Approx. 8 thick slices

Prep Time: 15 minutes

Cook Time: 40-45 minutes

Ingredients:

- 8oz/225g self-raising flour, plus level tsp of baking powder
- 8oz/225g cooked freekeh

- 2tsp baking soda
- 2 large eggs
- 8oz/225g pumpkin puree
- 2fl.oz/60ml olive oil
- 1tbsp molasses, or honey if you prefer
- 1tsp ground cinnamon
- 1tsp nutmeg
- 2tsp black onion seeds (nigella seeds) or mustard seeds
- Handful of pumpkin seeds
- 3oz/85g brown sugar
- 1tsp salt

Method:

You will need a 16oz/450g loaf tin, or a 20 x 20cm/8 x 8in baking dish.

Heat oven to 180°C/350°F/Gas mark 4.

Mix together all the dry ingredients – flour, freekeh, cinnamon, nutmeg, salt, brown sugar and onion seeds. In a separate bowl, mix together the wet ingredients – eggs, olive oil, molasses and pumpkin puree. Add the wet ingredients to the dry and gently mix together. The mixture should be of 'dropping consistency' and quite doughy. If for some reason it is a little wet, add some more flour.

Spoon the mixture into the loaf tin, press down gently, top with the pumpkin seeds and bake for 40-45 minutes, or until a knife inserted into the centre comes out clean. As ovens vary, don't be alarmed if you have to cook it for longer.

Serve with a steaming bowl of chilli, or if you prefer it with sweet accompaniments, you could pour honey over it, or even make it into French toast. Whichever way, this bread is absolutely delicious.

Tips:

This bread has been made so many times using seeds or nuts, chopped chillies and even jalapenos if you really like hot and spicy. Try varying the spices and using cumin or caraway seeds, fennel seeds etc. It really is worth experimenting.

Nutritional Analysis	Per slice
Carbohydrates	52g
of which sugars	14g
Total Fat	11g
of which saturates	3g
Fibre	5g
Sodium	.12g

DESSERTS AND SNACKS

Apricot Freekeh Dessert

This is a lovely dessert or treat, but can also be served for breakfast. Slightly Middle Eastern with the touch of cardamom and coconut milk, there is a delicious sweetness against the nutty flavour of the freekeh.

Serves: 4

Preparation Time: 5 minutes

Cook Time: 15-20 minutes

Ingredients:

- 7oz/200g freekeh
- 14oz/400g can of light coconut milk
- 8fl.oz/240ml of water
- 1tbsp ground cinnamon
- 1tsp ground cardamom
- 4tbsp brown rice syrup or agave syrup
- 4oz/115g canned apricots in natural juice, chopped (reserve the juice)
- 1tsp vanilla extract
- Large handful pistachios, chopped

Method:

Mix together the coconut milk and the water and pour into a saucepan. Add the freekeh and bring up to the boil for one minute.

Put all the other ingredients into the pan, excluding the nuts, and simmer for 15 minutes.

Just before removing from the heat, add some of the apricot juice to taste.

Serve in bowls, top with the chopped pistachios.

Nutritional Analysis	Per portion
Energy	456kcal
Protein	13.5g
Carbohydrates	52g
of which sugars	8g
Total Fat	23g
of which saturates	14g
Fibre	7g
Sodium	tr

Banana Freekeh Kisses

A wonderful lunchbox treat for the children, or for adults as well! Two different coatings, one with pine nuts (you can use chopped mixed nuts or other crushed nuts if preferred) and the other with a coconut coating. The hint of sweetness from the raw honey or agave syrup makes these treats very child friendly.

Serves: 10-12 kisses

Preparation Time: 10 minutes

Cook Time: 10-15 minutes until firm

Ingredients:

- 4oz/115g cooked freekeh, drained thoroughly
- 3 medium sized bananas, mashed
- ½tbsp raw honey or agave syrup
- 3oz/85g dessicated coconut
- 3oz/85g pine nuts or chopped nuts

Method:

Heat oven to 160°C/325°F/Gas mark 3

Line a baking sheet with parchment paper.

Mash the bananas really well, add the honey or syrup. Add the cooked freekeh.

The mixture will be quite wet, but persevere and roll the balls in the palm of your hand.

On a board, have the coconut on one side, and the nuts on the other. Roll each ball in your choice of coatings.

Place the balls on the baking sheet and bake in the oven for 10-12 minutes. They will feel quite soft, but they harden once they are cooled. Store in an airtight container in the fridge for up to 5 days.

Nutritional Analysis	Per Kiss
Energy	159 kcal
Protein	4g
Carbohydrates	11g
of which sugars	40g
Total Fat	10g
of which saturates	8g
Fibre	5g
Sodium	tr

Freekeh Blackberry and Apple Crumble

Everyone loves a fruit crumble, and as opposed to using flour in the crumble, we have used the lovely nutty freekeh. You can use any fruit you wish – in the winter, delicious anise spiced plums are wonderful and a real heart-warmer in the cold weather.

Serves: 4-5

Preparation Time: 10 minutes

Cook Time: 20-25 minutes

Ingredients:

For the crumble

- 5oz/140g freekeh, cooked, cooled and thoroughly drained
- 2oz/55g caster sugar
- 2oz/55g unsalted butter, softened

For the fruit compote

- 11oz/300g good quality apples
- 1oz/30g Demerara sugar
- 4oz/115g blackberries
- 1tsp nutmeg
- 1tsp cinnamon

Method:

Heat oven to 180°C/350°F/Gas mark 4

Tip the cooked freekeh into a large bowl and add the sugar and butter. Rub the mix together with your fingertips to make a nice crumbly texture (it may feel a little gritty in comparison to flour based crumble, but this is fine). Set aside.

Peel, core and cut the apples into 2cm/1inch dice. Put into a pan and cover with water. Add the cinnamon and nutmeg. Bring to the boil then simmer for about 5 minutes until softened but not mushy. Turn off the heat and drain the apples.

Put the apples into a bowl and mix in the blackberries, even though the apple will still be warm. If you are making the dessert in separate dishes, portion the fruit into each, alternatively, lay the fruit out in one baking dish.

Top the fruit with the crumble mix and bake in the oven for 20 minutes until bubbling and golden.

Serve with vanilla ice cream, double cream or custard – yum!

Nutritional Analysis	Per Portion
Energy	395kcals
Protein	4g
Carbohydrates	48g
Total Fat	19g
of which saturates	11g
Fibre	8g

Freekeh Pizza Margharita for the Kids!

This is a great 'cheats' pizza, using halved pitta bread, which is also a healthier dish and just as tasty. You can add whatever toppings you want, but we have kept it simple with cheese, tomato and ham. If your children love pineapple, a few chopped up pieces on the top really goes down well.

Serves: 4

Preparation Time: 10 minutes

Cook Time: 5-10 minutes

Ingredients:

- 2 pitta breads, sliced lengthways through the middle to form 4 oval shapes
- 4oz/115g freekeh, cooked
- 4tbsp tomato puree or red pesto
- 6 cherry tomatoes, quartered or 8 slices of tomato
- 12 slices of buffalo mozzarella

- 8 basil leaves, torn or shredded
- 4 thin slices of deli ham, rolled up and sliced

Method:

Heat oven to 180°C/350°F/Gas mark 4

Spread a tablespoon of puree or pesto on to each pitta slice.

Scatter the freekeh over each pitta, using your hands. Top with the ham, mozzarella and tomatoes and bake in the oven for 5-8 minutes until the mozzarella has melted.

Nutritional Analysis	Per Portion
Energy	318Kcals
Protein	20g
Carbohydrates	34g
of which sugars	5g
Total Fat	8g
of which saturates	6g
Fibre	5g
Sodium	.7g

Freekeh with Honey Roasted Figs and Ricotta

A lovely dish for a starter or as part of a buffet or a light lunch. A great combination of a rich freekeh base with herbs and a sweeter topping from the roasted figs, ricotta and honey. If not a vegetarian, add some crispy slices for a delicious accompaniment.

Serves: 4

Preparation Time: 5 minutes

Cook Time: 20 minutes

Ingredients:

- 5oz/140g freekeh
- 8 figs
- 3½oz/100g ricotta cheese
- 4tbsp honey
- 2tsp cinnamon
- 1tbsp fresh mint, chopped
- 2tbsp pine nuts
- 4 thin slices of pancetta or Parma ham, crisped under the grill

Method:

Heat the oven to 180°C/350°F/Gas mark 4

Cook the freekeh as per packet instructions. Meanwhile, gently criss-cross the figs at the stalk end, drizzle with a little honey and cinnamon. Bake in the oven for 15-20 minutes, depending on ripeness. Remove from the oven and keep warm.

Take the freekeh off the heat and if any remaining water, drain off. Mix the mint through the warm freekeh and set aside, covered to keep in the heat.

Heat the grill to full power and crisp up the pancetta or Parma ham. Remove from the grill.

Portion the freekeh on plates or bowls. Split the figs open a little more if still slightly closed, and put a half a tablespoon of ricotta into the fig. Top with a little more honey and pine nuts.

If you are using the pancetta or Parma, you can serve the slices whole, or crumble up over the dish.

Nutritional Analysis	Per Portion
Energy	451kcal
Protein	14g
Carbohydrates	39g
of which sugars	25g
Total Fat	17g
of which saturates	12g
Fibre	9g
Sodium	.2mg

Wholesome Freekeh Vegetable Stew

A great autumn or winter warmer on a cold and blustery or wet day and packed with vitamins to keep infections away. Kale is a 'superfood' and can be much ignored as an addition to soups and stews.

Serves: 4-6

Preparation Time: 10 minutes

Cook Time: 45-50 minutes

Ingredients:

- 6oz/170g uncooked freekeh, rinsed
- 2tbsp olive oil
- 1 large onion, chopped
- 1 large leek, dark green ends removed, and chopped
- 2 medium sized sweet potatoes, peeled and diced
- 3 celery sticks, finely sliced
- ½ bunch of kale, finely shredded
- 1tbsp garam massala
- 1tsp ground cumin
- 1tsp fresh coriander, finely chopped
- 28fl.oz/1½ pints vegetable stock or broth
- Seasoning to taste

Method:

In a large pot, heat the oil on medium heat and add the onions, sweet potatoes, celery and leeks. Stir until the vegetables have begun to soften.

Add the cumin and garam massala and stir to coat all the vegetables, about 2 minutes.

Stir in the freekeh and add the vegetable stock. Bring to the boil then reduce to simmer for 20 minutes.

Add the kale, taste and season the stew.

Cover and cook for a further 10 minutes until the stew has reduced a little and all the vegetables are tender. Divide into portions and sprinkle over the fresh coriander.

Serve with some crusty bread to mop up the juices!

Nutritional Analysis	Per Portion (4)
Energy	296kcal
Protein	10g
Carbohydrates	43g
of which sugars	10g
Total Fat	10g
of which saturates	2g
Fibre	8g
Sodium	98g

DINNERS

Beef Stroganoff with Minted Pea Freekeh

Succulent and tender beef strips with mushrooms and shallots, accompany a dish of freekeh and minted peas, a different twist for the freekeh. You can use the pea variation of the freekeh with most meats or fish, but if mint is not on your list of foods to love, you can substitute it for parsley – but the mint is lovely and fresh against the cream sauce.

Serves: 4

Preparation Time: 15 minutes

Cook Time: 15-20 minutes

Ingredients:

- 1lb/450g lean rump steak, kept as cold as possible
- 7oz/200g freekeh
- 1tbsp olive oil
- 1tbsp butter
- 11oz/300g button mushrooms
- 3 shallots or 1 red onion, finely chopped
- 1tbsp plain flour
- 10fl.oz/300ml beef stock
- 1½tbsp Dijon mustard

- 1tbsp tomato puree
- 3tbsp crème fraiche or sour cream
- 3½oz/100g frozen peas
- 1tbsp fresh mint, chopped
- Seasoning to taste

Method:

Keep the beef as cold as possible, you can even freeze it for 30 minutes. Finely slice into strips and season with a little salt and pepper.

In a large frying pan, heat the oil and quickly sear the beef on all sides. Remove from the pan and set aside.

To the same pan, add the shallots and mushrooms, fry until softened. Place with the beef.

Cook the freekeh as per packet instructions for approximately 15 minutes. Just before removing from the heat, add the peas and stir.

While the freekeh is cooking, add the butter to the pan, stir in the flour to form a paste (roux) and gradually add the beef stock. Continue to mix whilst adding the stock.

Bubble until thickened, then add the crème fraiche and a little more seasoning. Add the beef and mushroom/shallot mixture and continue to stir.

Drain the freekeh and pea mixture and add ¾ of the mint. Serve either in a separate bowl or with the stroganoff on top. Scatter the beef with remaining mint or if you prefer, parsley.

Nutritional Analysis	Per Portion
Energy	602kcal
Protein	48g
Carbohydrates	43g
of which sugars	4g
Total Fat	23g
of which saturates	9g
Fibre	8g
Sodium	3g

Chilli Con Carne with Freekeh

There is nothing like a warming bowl of chilli on a cold autumn or winters' night, and as opposed to rice, try having freekeh as the accompaniment. Its' nutty texture is a nice change to the usual steamed or boiled rice – you could also mix peas or corn through the rice for another texture. Try making the chilli the day before, so that all the spices have time to infuse.

Serves: 4

Preparation Time: 15 minutes

Cook Time: 30 minutes (the longer the chilli is left, the deeper the flavour)

Ingredients:

- 1tbsp olive oil
- 1 large onion, finely diced
- 2 cloves garlic, finely chopped
- 1 heaped tsp hot chilli powder
- 1tsp paprika
- 1tsp ground cumin
- 1lb/450g lean minced beef
- 1 beef stock cube
- 1lb/450g can chopped tomatoes
- 1tsp sugar
- 2tbsp tomato puree
- 1lb/450g can red kidney beans
- 7oz/200g freekeh
- A little water, if required
- Seasoning to taste

Method:

Heat the oil until hot, add the onions and fry for 3-4 minutes, until soft and almost translucent. Add the garlic, chilli powder, paprika and cumin and stir. Leave for 5 minutes, stirring occasionally to combine.

In a separate pan, brown the mince, making sure you break up the mince so that there are no lumps. Add the mince to the onion mixture and add the chopped tomatoes and tomato puree. Add the sugar and stir. Adjust the seasoning as required, place a lid over the pan and simmer for 10-15 minutes. If the mixture becomes a little dry, add some water. After 10 minutes, add the kidney beans.

Replace the lid, turn off the heat and leave to stand for 10 minutes.

Make sure you stir the mix from time to time to prevent burning or sticking. Whilst the chilli is cooking, place the freekeh in a pan and cook as per packet instructions for 15-20 minutes.

Drain the freekeh and serve with the chilli, perhaps with some garlic bread or a tossed green salad.

Nutritional Analysis	Per Portion
Energy	652kcal
Protein	53g
Carbohydrates	59g
of which sugars	8g
Total Fat	21g
of which saturates	7g
Fibre	16g
Sodium	3g

Easy Freekeh Lamb Biryani

You can use leftover leg of lamb for this dish, or alternatively use lamb neck fillet, which is tender and quick to cook. This tasty all in one dish benefits from accompaniments of cucumber and mint raita, and fresh sliced mango – very refreshing. You could also serve this with warm naan bread, or chapatis.

Serves: 4

Preparation Time: 10 minutes

Cook Time: 30 minutes

Ingredients:

- 1tbsp vegetable oil
- 1lb/450g lamb neck fillet
- 1 large white onion
- 3tbsp balti curry paste
- 13fl.oz/400ml lamb stock (you can use chicken stock)
- 9oz/250g freekeh
- 2 handfuls of baby spinach
- Handful of sultanas
- 2tbsp fresh coriander, chopped
- 1 mango, peeled and sliced (stone removed)

For the Raita

- 2inches/5cm cucumber, skin and seeds removed, diced
- 7oz/200g plain thick yoghurt
- 1tbsp fresh mint, finely chopped

Method:

Mix together all the ingredients for the raita in a small bowl. Set aside.

Over a low heat, lightly sauté the onions in the oil. Add the curry paste and continue to soften the onions in the paste.

Add the lamb*, and brown on all sides, mixing thoroughly with the onions and curry paste.

Add the stock and the freekeh and bring to the boil, covered with a lid. Continue to cook for approximately 15 minutes until the freekeh is soft and the lamb is tender. Turn off the heat, add the spinach (if desired), replace the lid and leave to steam for 5 minutes.

Stir through the sultanas, portion into bowls and top with the coriander. Some flaked almonds are also tasty with this dish.

Serve with the raita and Indian bread. Top with mango slices or place in a separate dish.

<u>*If using leftover lamb, put in the lamb at the end of the boiling period.</u>

Nutritional Analysis	Per Portion
Energy	600kcal
Protein	41g
Carbohydrates	50g
of which sugars	12g
Total Fat	27g
of which saturates	11g
Fibre	7g
Sodium	.1g

Freekeh Mushroom and Herb Pilaff

This is a relatively quick pilaff to make, and you can also add 'leftovers' such as chopped chicken, beef or lamb if you have some available from a roasted joint of meat. We have used a combination of mushrooms to give the pilaff different textures and depths of flavour, as standard mushrooms these days sometimes don't have much flavour.

Serves: 4

Preparation Time: 10 minutes

Cook Time: 20-25 minutes

Ingredients:

- 7oz/200g freekeh
- 2 onions, sliced very thinly
- 5oz/140g mixed mushrooms such as chestnut, button, field, shitake etc
- 1oz/25g butter
- 2tbsp olive oil
- 1tsp ground allspice
- 12fl.oz/350ml vegetable stock
- 2tsp fresh lemon juice

- 2 garlic cloves, crushed
- Small handful fresh parsley, chopped
- Small handful fresh mint, chopped
- 2tbsp chopped nuts, such as almonds or pine nuts
- Seasoning to taste
- 3½oz/100g Greek yoghurt (add a little chopped cucumber and chopped mint, it makes a difference)

Method:

Gently sauté the onions in half of the olive oil. When softened, add the mushrooms.

Cook the freekeh in the stock until all the liquid has been absorbed. Add the freekeh to the mushroom and onion mix, along with the garlic, spices (if you are using meat, add at this time). Stir and heat gently.

Mix in the fresh herbs, reserving a little for decoration on the top. Season to taste and place a lid over the pilaff to keep warm.

Mix together the yoghurt, mint and cucumber in a bowl.

When ready to serve, sprinkle over the chopped nuts and any remaining herbs and the olive oil.

Nutritional Analysis	Per Portion
Energy	474kcal
Protein	22g
Carbohydrates	38g
of which sugars	4g
Total Fat	27g
of which saturates	7g
Fibre	7g
Sodium	2g

Freekeh Sausage and Chips for Little Ones!

These little sausage shaped delights will surely be loved by the little members of the family and are healthier than the usual sausages, as they have no skin on them. Oven baked chips lightly coated in olive oil are also a healthier version. You could use sweet potatoes instead of ordinary potatoes, to make the dish even healthier.

Serves: 4 little ones!

Preparation Time: 10 minutes

Cook Time: 25-30 minutes

Ingredients:

For the sausages

- 4oz/115g lean minced pork
- 6oz/170g freekeh, cooked
- 1 small red pepper, very finely chopped
- ½ small onion, minced
- 1tbsp flour for coating
- Seasoning to taste

For the chips

- 2 large potatoes, washed but skin left on and cut into thin wedges
- ½tbsp olive oil
- 1tsp Cajun seasoning

Method:

Heat oven to 180°C/350°F/Gas mark 4.

Mix the minced pork, freekeh, pepper and onion together, and season to taste.

Mix together the oil and the Cajun seasoning in a bowl, and toss the chips around in the oil. Line a baking sheet and spread the chips out.

Spread the flour onto a chopping board, and shape the pork mix into a large ball in the palm of your hand, and then roll into a 'sausage shape' to coat in the flour.

Place the chips in the oven on the top shelf, and the sausages on another baking tray on the second shelf. After 15 minutes, turn both the chips and the sausages over. Bake for a further 15 minutes until golden. As ovens vary, it may take a little longer to cook.

Nutritional Analysis	Per
Energy	290Kcal
Protein	17g
Carbohydrates	32g
of which sugars	5g
Total Fat	19g
of which saturates	8g
Fibre	3g
Sodium	1g

Freekeh Shrimp Gumbo

A delicious taste of the Southern US States, the freekeh is a substitute for the usual rice that is served with traditional gumbo, and probably more like a paella style dish. Very tasty and a little spicy with the Cajun influence.

Serves: 6

Preparation Time: 10 minutes

Cook Time: 30 minutes

Ingredients:

- 9oz/250g freekeh
- 4oz/115g canned sweetcorn, drained
- 18 large raw shrimp (3 per person, but by all means use more)
- 2tbsp olive oil
- 4tbsp Cajun Seasoning
- 1tsp hot chilli powder
- 3 cloves garlic, crushed
- 1 red and 1 green pepper, cored, seeds removed and roughly chopped
- 2 onions, sliced
- 1lb/450g can chopped tomatoes
- 2 sticks celery, chopped
- 2 low sodium chicken stock cubes

- 2tbsp scallion 'tips' (the green part) finely chopped
- Water (if the gumbo begins to dry out)

Method:

Cook the freekeh with the celery in the required amount of water as per packet instructions.

Meanwhile, clean the shrimp. Place in a bowl with the crushed garlic, Cajun seasoning and half the olive oil. Mix to coat the prawns.

Cook the onions, peppers in a little oil until slightly tender. Set aside.

Heat the remaining oil on a medium heat, and throw the shrimp and the marinade into the pan. Cook until the shrimps are pink. Put the peppers and onion mix back into the pan and stir over a low heat. Add the tomatoes, stock cubes and chilli powder and cook on simmer. Add a little water if the mix begins to dry out.

Just before serving, add the drained sweetcorn to the shrimp mix. Serve the gumbo with the freekeh on one side, sprinkled with the scallion tips.

Nutritional Analysis	Per Portion
Energy	285kcal
Protein	23g
Carbohydrates	33g
of which sugars	7g
Total Fat	8g
of which saturates	3g
Fibre	6g
Sodium	.3g

Freekeh Vegetable Bake

This dish can either be made as an accompaniment to fish or meat, or as a stand alone dish with a tasty mixed salad and some good crusty bread such as a baguette or ciabatta. Either way, it's quite quick to make and tastes delicious. The vegetables can be any that you choose, but we have tended to use Mediterranean vegetables for colour and texture, as well as flavour.

Serves: 4

Preparation Time: 10 minutes

Cook Time: 30 minutes

Ingredients:

- 2tbs olive oil
- 1 large aubergine, sliced into rounds
- 6oz/170g mushrooms, sliced
- 1 red and 1 green pepper, deseeded and sliced
- 2 cloves garlic, finely chopped or crushed
- 7oz/200g freekeh, cooked
- 4 or 5 sundried tomatoes, roughly chopped
- Handful of fresh mixed herbs, such as rosemary, parsley, thyme, chopped
- 3tbsp single cream, or if preferred crème fraiche
- 4oz/115g cheddar cheese, grated

Method:

Heat oven to 180°C/350°F/Gas mark 4

Heat the oil in a pan over medium heat, and fry the aubergine for 3 or 4 minutes each side until golden and cooked through. Set aside.

Fry the mushrooms, peppers, onions, garlic over a medium heat until softened, adding a little more oil if necessary. Add the freekeh and mix together. Add the herbs and sun dried tomatoes, and any seasoning you require.

Add the cream, and bring the dish back to just before boiling, to heat through. Turn off the heat.

Place the aubergines in the bottom of a baking dish and pour over the freekeh vegetable mix. Top with the grated cheese and place in the oven for 10-15 until golden and bubbly, probably about 10-15 minutes.

Serve with a mixed leaf salad and some crusty bread if a main meal.

Nutritional Analysis	Per Portion
Energy	419kcal
Protein	18g
Carbohydrates	38g
of which sugars	6g
Total Fat	23g
of which saturates	7g
Fibre	9g
Sodium	.2g

Herb Crusted Salmon with Spinach Freekeh

Rich in Omega 3, Salmon is one of the best fish that you can eat. Coated in fresh herbs and lemon, baked in foil in the oven, you can make this dish and be ready to eat it in under 25 minutes! Try serving with some more steamed greens or roasted tomatoes.

Serves: 4

Preparation Time: 5 minutes

Cook Time: 15-20 minutes

Ingredients:

- 6oz/170g freekeh
- Large handful of baby spinach
- 4 x 5oz/140g salmon fillets
- Juice and grated rind of 1 lemon
- 1 lemon, quartered for garnish
- 4 parsley stems, leaves removed and chopped
- 4 chives, finely chopped
- 1tsp ground nutmeg
- 3oz/85g brown breadcrumbs
- Freshly milled black pepper

Method:

Heat oven to 180°C/350°F/Gas mark 4

Prepare the breadcrumbs in your food processor and set aside. Prepare 4 pieces of foil, large enough to make parcels for the salmon.

Mix chives, parsley and lemon juice with the breadcrumbs. Add some freshly milled black pepper to taste.

Coat the salmon fillets in the breadcrumb mix and place each one onto the foil. Bring the sides together, fold over the top of the salmon and close the edges. Place in the oven.

Meanwhile, cook the freekeh for 15 minutes in a saucepan (one that has a lid). After 15 minutes, add the spinach and nutmeg, stir and place the lid on. Turn off the heat.

Check that the salmon fillets have turned a pale pink and are juicy. Leave the packets open and turn off the oven. Keep warm.

Serve the freekeh onto plates, and top with the salmon. Choose your own choice of steamed vegetables or salad to accompany.

Nutritional Analysis	Per Portion
Energy	260kcal
Protein	22g
Carbohydrates	36g
of which sugars	2g
Total Fat	6g
of which saturates	1g
Fibre	7g
Sodium	.2g

Maple Roasted Chicken with Freekeh Stuffing

A lovely change from the usual roast chicken Sunday lunch. Freekeh makes a very different and welcome change to normal stuffings, as it is nuttier in texture and combines well with herbs and almost any ingredient you want to stuff your chicken with. Here is a suggestion, but please do experiment.

Serves: 4

Preparation Time: 15 minutes

Cook Time: 90 minutes

Ingredients:

For the chicken

- 1 large free range chicken
- 3tbsp maple syrup
- 2tsp mild mustard
- 1tbsp olive oil

For the stuffing

- 3½oz/100g freekeh, cooked
- ½ orange, peeled and cut into small pieces

- ½ onion, finely chopped
- 2tbsp fresh parsley, finely chopped
- 2 garlic cloves, crushed
- Handful of dried cranberries
- 1tsp dried cinnamon
- Seasoning to taste

Method:

Heat oven to 180°C/350°F/Gas mark 4.

In a bowl, mix together all the stuffing ingredients and add seasoning to taste. If too dry, add a little water.

Make sure the chicken is clean both outside and inside the cavity. Wipe dry with paper towel.

Fill the chicken with the stuffing mix and tie the legs together to prevent too much spilling out. If there is any remaining stuffing, place in a dish, cover with foil and set aside.

Mix the olive oil, maple syrup and mustard together, and rub all over the chicken.

Roast the chicken for 1 hour and 20 minutes. Test to see if cooked through by inserting the tip of a sharp knife just above the leg – the juices should run clear.

Any remaining stuffing can be placed in the oven in the covered dish and reheated for about 10 minutes.

Serve the chicken cut into slices or joints with perhaps some roasted carrots and parsnips.

Nutritional Analysis	Per portion
Energy	389kcal
Protein	48g
Carbohydrates	18g
of which sugars	3g
Total Fat	14g
of which saturates	4g
Fibre	4g
Sodium	.03g

Marvellous Freekeh Meatloaf

This is a great dinner party dish or a dish that can last you for a few days if you are eating solo! It takes a little bit of effort, but the results are worthwhile and the leftovers delicious hot or cold. You will need a 2lb/1kg non-stick loaf tin to hold the mixture. You could also use minced chicken, turkey or pork in this recipe.

Serves: 8-10 slices
Preparation Time: 10 minutes
Cook Time: 50 mins-1 hour

Ingredients:

- 14oz/390g cooked freekeh
- 1lb/450g of extra-lean minced or ground beef
- 2 celery sticks, finely diced
- 2 red onions, finely chopped
- 4 cloves of garlic, crushed or finely chopped
- 1tbsp fresh parsley, chopped
- 1tbsp fresh coriander, chopped
- 2 Omega 3 eggs, beaten
- 8 rashers of lean bacon or pancetta (this can be left out if required)
- Seasoning to taste

Method:

Heat the oven to 160°C/325°F/Gas mark 3.

In a large bowl, mix all the ingredients together, excluding the bacon.

Line the loaf tin with the bacon rashers, leaving a slight overlap at the top. Using a large spoon, put all the mixture, or as much as you can, up to the top of the tin. Fold the bacon overlap over the mixture. Press down on the meatloaf to make it a little more compact.

Bake in the oven for 50 minutes, test with a skewer to ensure the meatloaf is cooked through – the skewer should come out relatively clean.

Remove from the oven and leave to cool for 10 minutes. Once cooled, tip out any excess liquid. Turn the meatloaf out, using a plate on the top and flipping over.

Serve with a mixed salad or vegetables. If you have any leftover meat mixture, roll into balls and freeze for a tasty snack.

Nutritional Analysis	Per Slice
Energy	245kcal
Protein	19g
Carbohydrates	15g
of which sugars	2g
Total Fat	11g
of which saturates	6g
Fibre	27g
Sodium	.4g

Mediterranean Freekeh Stuffed Peppers

The deep and rich flavour of the Mediterranean is reflected in this really easy to make dish. It serves as a wonderful starter, but can equally be double up and served as a main course with a tossed green salad and a garlic vinaigrette. There are many combinations that are a good match for this sunshine dish.

Serves: 4 starter portions

Preparation time: 20 minutes

Cooking time: 20 minutes

Ingredients:

- 6oz/170g freekeh, cooked
- 1 large red, and 1 large yellow pepper, halved, but leave stalks on, seeds and core removed
- 3oz/85g feta cheese, crumbled
- Handful cherry tomatoes, quartered (Can use semi dried tomatoes)
- 2oz/55g pine nuts, toasted
- Handful black olives, roughly chopped
- 2tbsp shredded basil
- Ground black pepper to season
- Drizzle of olive oil for each pepper

Method:

Cook the freekeh as per packet instructions.

Heat oven to 200°C/400°F/gas mark 6.

Put the peppers on a plate and microwave on medium for around 5 minutes, until almost soft. Place on a baking tray, cut-side up. Mix the freekeh with the olives, feta, pine nuts, tomatoes and basil.

Load the freekeh stuffing into the pepper halves and bake for around 10-12 minutes.

Serve with a little ground black pepper on the top, a little drizzle of olive oil, and some crusty bread to soak up the juices!

Nutritional Analysis	Per Portion
Energy	210kcal
Protein	12g
Carbohydrates	20g
of which sugars	2g
Total Fat	18g
of which saturates	10g
Fibre	4g
Sodium	.3g

Mexican Beef and Freekeh Pizza

Another pizza style dish, this time using a thicker coriander and garlic flatbread and topping with minced beef and fajita or chilli seasoning. Really quick and easy to make.

Serves: 2

Preparation Time: 5 minutes

Cook Time: 20 minutes (more if you want the beef to marinate more)

Ingredients:

- 6oz/170g lean minced beef or steak
- 6oz/170g freekeh, cooked
- 2 flatbreads
- 1 onion, diced
- 1 sachet or 2tbsp taco or fajita seasoning
- 1tbsp tomato puree
- 2 cloves garlic, crushed
- 1tsp fresh coriander, chopped
- 1tbsp vegetable oil
- 2tbsp guacamole, either shop bought or homemade
- Sour cream if desired

Method:

Heat oven to 180°C/350F°/Gas Mark 4.

Pan fry the onions and garlic until soft and slightly coloured. Remove from the pan and set aside.

In the same pan, gently fry the mince with the taco or fajita seasoning. When the meat is cooked through and browned, add the onions back into the pan and add the tomato puree and cooked freekeh. Mix to combine everything together. Remove the pan from the heat.

Heat the flat bread or naan bread for 5-8 minutes. Reheat the minced beef mixture until completely warmed through. Serve on the bread with guacamole and/or sour cream and salad.

Nutritional Analysis	Per
Energy	510kcals
Protein	24g
Carbohydrates	46g
of which sugars	19g
Total Fat	38g
of which saturates	21g
Fibre	6g
Sodium	.9g

Roasted Root Vegetables with Freekeh

You can use any root vegetables and other vegetables in this dish depending how filling you want it to be and as long as you gauge the cooking time of non-root vegetables. We have used baby asparagus in this dish, which only needs to be put in for the last 10-15 minutes of cooking.

Serves: 4

Preparation Time: 10 minutes

Cook Time: 45 minutes

Ingredients:

- 2 medium sized sweet potatoes, cut into 2 inch/5cm chunks
- 2 medium sized parsnips, quartered and then halved
- ½ small swede, cut into 2 inch/5cm chunks
- 1 large red onion, cut into wedges
- 8 baby asparagus spears
- 2tbsp olive oil
- 8oz/225g freekeh, cooked
- Seasoning to taste
- 1tbsp maple or agave syrup

Method:

Heat oven to 180°C/350°F/Gas mark 4

Put the oil and maple/agave syrup into a large bowl and mix all the vegetables into the mix making sure they are all coated. Season.

Put the vegetables excluding the asparagus into a large enough baking tray and place in the oven.

Cook for 30 minutes and then toss in the asparagus and mix the vegetables around again. Cook for a further 15 minutes until vegetables are all tender. Ovens do vary, so if the dish needs more time, don't worry. 5 minutes before the vegetables are ready, mix in the freekeh and cook the whole dish together, or alternatively, reheat the freekeh in the microwave for 2 minutes, spread out on a serving dish and top with the vegetables.

Nutritional Analysis	Per Portion
Energy	335kcal
Protein	12g
Carbohydrates	54g
of which sugars	10g
Total Fat	10g
of which saturates	1g
Fibre	9g
Sodium	.05g

Roasted Vegetable Freekeh Soup

As bad as it seems to say, most of the freekeh soup recipes we have come across seem quite bland, and certainly not attractive to the eye. So we set out to come up with a much more flavoursome soup, that you could be immediately attracted to once looked at. Roasting vegetables obviously increases the flavour of the majority of vegetables, so this is what we came up with. This soup will freeze, so try to make a batch of it.

Serves: 3-4 as a starter portion

Preparation Time: 20 minutes

Cook Time: 45 minutes, including roasting the vegetables

Ingredients:

- 4oz/115g freekeh, cooked
- 3 red peppers, deseeded and cut into small chunks
- 2 onions, diced
- 6 tomatoes
- 3 carrots, peeled and cut into small chunks
- 6oz/170g pumpkin (weight less hard skin)
- 1 tsp chilli powder
- Salt and freshly ground black pepper

- 2 chicken stock cubes (you can use vegetable stock if required)
- 16fl.oz/1 pint of water
- 1tbsp olive oil
- 1tsp sumac

Method:

Heat the oven to 180°C/350°F/Gas mark 4

Put all the vegetables into a roasting tray with the olive oil and sumac, and roast for 40 minutes.

When roasted, remove the skin from the pumpkin, and place all the vegetables in a liquidiser and blitz until a rough mixture. Push through a sieve to remove any skins etc from the mixture.

Pour into a saucepan with half the water, and add the cooked freekeh, stock cubes and chilli powder. Bring to the boil, and then simmer to reduce the liquid. Once starting to thicken, continue to add the water a little at a time.

Season to taste, serve with warm bread or crackers.

Nutritional Analysis	Per portion
Energy	173kcal
Protein	7g
Carbohydrates	26g
of which sugars	8g
Total Fat	22g
of which saturates	1g
Fibre	6g
Sodium	.06mg

Roasted Balsamic Beets with Freekeh and Yoghurt

Roasted beets are delicious when drizzled with olive oil and balsamic and a wonderful healthy accompaniment to freekeh. A spoonful of Greek yoghurt or some crumbled goats cheese on the top provides a delicious all round meal.

Serves: 4

Preparation Time: 10 minutes

Cook Time: 45 minutes

Ingredients:

- 8 medium sized beets
- 2tbsp balsamic vinegar
- 1tbsp runny honey
- 1tsp fresh thyme, leaves chopped
- 2tbsp olive oil
- 7oz/200g freekeh
- 4 heaped tbsp Greek yoghurt or crumbled goats cheese
- Rocket or mixed leaves to serve

Method:

Heat oven to 180°C/350°F/Gas mark 4

Trim the leaves and most of the stalk off the beets. Boil in water for approximately 10 minutes, leave to cool and remove skin and any stalk.

Mix the balsamic, olive oil, thyme and honey together. Mix the beets with the dressing.

Roast the beets in a tray in the oven for 30 minutes. After 15 minutes, cook the freekeh in water for 15-20 minutes, so that the freekeh is ready at the same time.

Drain the freekeh, top with the beets (halved or quartered depending on size) and a generous dollop of yoghurt or crumbled goats cheese.

Serve with rocket leaves or salad and seasoning.

Nutritional Analysis	Per Portion
Energy	296kcal
Protein	11g
Carbohydrates	44g
of which sugars	11g
Total Fat	10g
of which saturates	4g
Fibre	7g
Sodium	.07g

Slow Cooked Pork and Lentil Casserole with Apple and Freekeh

This meal goes a long way for a small budget, warming and delicious - perfect for a winter supper. Economical cuts of pork can be used, including pork shoulder, but remember to remove any excess fat. Slow cookers or crockpots do vary nowadays, some cooking at a much higher heat than others, particularly the latest ones. It is advisable to check the consistency of your ingredients in the pot a few times, so that they do not disintegrate too much.

Serves: 4

Preparation Time: 15 minutes

Cook Time: 6-8 hours

Ingredients:

- 6 sticks celery, washed and chopped,
- 2 medium sized onions diced
- 1lb/450g pork, diced into 2 inch/5cm cubes
- 1lb/450g cooking apples, peeled, cored and quartered
- 3 carrots peeled and batoned
- 2 parsnips peeled and sliced thickly
- 18fl.oz/500ml apple juice
- 18fl.oz/500ml good chicken or vegetable stock
- 3½oz/100g puy lentils, rinsed and picked over for any stones
- 3½oz/100g freekeh
- 1 tablespoon sunflower oil

Method:

Heat the oil and toss the meat, celery carrots and onions together in a large pan for 3 or 4 minutes until the meat is lightly browned and the celery, carrots and onions are slightly softened. Place into a crockpot or slow cooker.

Add the lentils, freekeh, stock and apple juice and stir together making sure the meat, freekeh and lentils are submerged in the stock.

Place on the high setting and cook for 4-5 hours, then check the consistency of the ingredients. If they are becoming quite soft (all slow cookers vary) turn to medium heat or even to simmer.

Add the apples and cook for a further 2 hours and test again. Repeat this after an hour if the ingredients, particularly the freekeh are still resistant.

Taste for seasoning before serving. Adjust as required.

Serve in dishes with crusty bread and spring greens or purple sprouting broccoli.

Nutritional Analysis	Per Portion
Energy	213kcal
Protein	20g
Carbohydrates	14g
of which sugars	6g
Total Fat	8g
of which saturates	2g
Fibre	8g
Sodium	0.3g

Spicy Freekeh Veggie Burgers

These burgers or patties seem to go down very well with non-vegetarians as well as those who choose a vegetarian lifestyle. Perhaps it's the combination of spices that lift these burgers up to a new level, as opposed to the very boring shop bought veggie burgers – who knows, but it works!

Serves: 6 medium sized burgers

Preparation Time: 20 minutes

Cook Time: 10 minutes

Ingredients:

- 7oz/200g freekeh, cooked
- 1 large onion, finely diced
- 1 medium sized courgette, grated and some of the moisture squeezed out
- 1 medium sized carrot, grated and some of the moisture squeezed out
- 1 small can (7oz/200g) chickpeas
- 1tbsp coriander, chopped
- 3 cloves garlic, crushed
- 2tbsp mild mustard
- 2tsp mild chilli powder
- 1tbsp mustard seeds
- 1 egg
- Brown rice flour to coat the burgers (approx 3oz/85g)
- 2tbsp rapeseed oil, for frying
- Juice of 1 lemon

Method:

In a liquidiser, or by hand if you feel strong enough, blitz or crush the chickpeas.

In a large bowl, mix the cooked freekeh and all of the vegetables, herbs and spices and chicken peas together. Beat the egg and add to the mixture, stirring to combine everything together.

On a clean board, sprinkle the flour. Shape the burgers into balls, then flatten out to burger shape. Coat in the flour.

You may need a little more flour on the board and on your hands to prevent the mixture from sticking, but don't overdue the flour coating.

Put the oil into a frying pan and heat gently. Place the burgers into the frying pan (probably best in 2 batches) and cook on either side for 3-4 minutes. The burgers should be lightly browned on each side, and beginning to crisp a little, due to the flour. You may need to add a little more oil for the second batch.

If cooked in two batches, place the first batch on a plate and cover with foil. Place in the oven at a low heat to keep warm.

Try serving with oven cooked sweet potato wedges, or of course, a delicious bun with salad.

Nutritional Analysis	Per burger
Energy	201kcal
Protein	9g
Carbohydrates	34g
of which sugars	4g
Total Fat	2g
of which saturates	1g
Fibre	4g
Sodium	.2g

Succulent Beef Freekeh Olives

Beef olives (there are no olives in this dish, in spite of the name!) braised in a red wine and tomato stock are truly delicious. You can vary the stuffing of the beef with other ingredients that you may like, but this one works really well. Simply double, treble the ingredients etc., to feed larger parties.

Serves: 2

Preparation Time: 10 minutes

Cook Time: 1 hour 20 minutes

Ingredients:

- 4 x 3½oz/100g slices of lean beef (minute steaks are a good choice), pounded out
- 4oz/115g cooked freekeh
- 1tbsp strong mustard
- 1 medium onion, finely chopped
- 4 or 5 mushrooms, finely chopped
- 1 stick of celery, finely chopped
- 1 garlic clove, finely chopped
- 1tbsp olive oil
- a few baby spinach leaves
- a small handful of pine nuts

For the sauce

- 14fl.oz/400ml beef stock
- 2-3tbsp tomato puree or passata
- 5fl.oz/150ml red wine
- 1tbsp rosemary, leaves only, chopped

Method:

Heat oven to 160°C/325°F/Gas Mark 3. Lightly 'bash' out each piece of beef so that they are about a couple of millimetres/¼inch thick. Brush each piece with mustard.

In a pan, gently fry off the onions, mushrooms, garlic and celery until soft. Add the spinach and pine nuts and freekeh and stir together. Starting at one edge, divide the filling between each of the slices, and roll tightly to a cylinder. Use cocktail sticks to keep the roll together. Place in a baking dish.

Mix the red wine and stock in a pan and bring to the boil, then simmer for 5 minutes. Add the tomato puree/passata and the rosemary and simmer for a further 5 minutes.

Pour the sauce over the beef, and cook in the oven for 45 minutes – 1 hour, covered in foil to prevent burning.

Serve with fresh seasonal vegetables.

Nutritional Analysis	Per portion
Energy	478kcal
Protein	30g
Carbohydrates	43g
of which sugars	4g
Total Fat	21g
of which saturates	3g
Fibre	8g
Sodium	1.7g

Sweet and Sour Chicken with Freekeh

Sweet and sour chicken is a great dish for small numbers or large and most children like it too! Rather than buy shop bought sauce, make your own, you may well have the items you need in your store cupboard.

Serves: 4

Preparation Time: 10 minutes

Cook Time: 25-30 minutes

Ingredients:

- 2tbsp vegetable oil or canola oil
- 14oz/390g freekeh
- 9tbsp good quality tomato ketchup
- 3tbp white wine vinegar
- 4tbsp muscovado sugar
- 2 cloves garlic, crushed
- 4 boneless and skinless chicken breasts, cut into medium sized chunks
- 1 onion, roughly chopped
- 1 red and 1 green pepper, seeds removed and cut into chunks

- 8oz/225g can of pineapple pieces in natural juice, drained (reserve 3tbsp for the sauce)
- 3½oz/100g sugar snap peas or mange tout

2Method:

Cook the freekeh as per packet instructions (about 15 mins) and keep warm

In the meantime, mix together the tomato ketchup, vinegar, sugar and 3 tbsp of the pineapple juice. Bring to the boil and leave to simmer for 5-6 minutes.

In a wok or a large frying pan on a medium heat, add a little oil and pan fry the chicken until cooked through, turning over every so often to keep the cooking even. Remove from the pan and set aside.

Add a little more oil and sauté the garlic, onions, peppers and peas until softened but still with a little crunch. Add the chicken back into the pan and continue to stir until combined. Mix in the pineapple.

Add the sweet and sour sauce, combine thoroughly, and bring up the heat so that the dish is almost bubbling.

Portion the freekeh onto plates, and top with the chicken mix.

You could add a few chopped scallions to the top when serving.

Nutritional Analysis	Per portion
Energy	325 kcal
Protein	38g
Carbohydrates	27g
Of which sugars	9g
Total Fat	3g
of which saturates	1g
Fibre	5g
Sodium	.09g

Tofu and Freekeh Vegetable Stir Fry

A healthy stir fry using tofu (try to get marinated tofu if you can, it has more flavour). Broccoli is a superfood and delicious when cooked and retaining a slight crunch. Overall a very quick and nutritious dish.

Serves: 4/5

Preparation Time: 10 minutes

Cook Time: 15 minutes

Ingredients:

- 1tbsp vegetable oil
- 1 head of broccoli, cut into florets
- 3 cloves garlic, finely sliced
- 1 red pepper, finely sliced
- 1 bunch scallions, diagonally sliced in 1 inch/2cm pieces
- 2 pak choi, roughly chopped
- Large handful sugar snap peas or mange tout
- 11oz/300g tofu
- 2tbsp hoisin sauce
- 1tbsp low-sodium light soy sauce
- 1oz/30g cashew nuts
- 7oz/200g freekeh, cooked

Method:

Cook freekeh as per packet instructions (15-20 minutes) drain and set aside.

Heat oil in a large frying pan and add the broccoli. Stir fry on a high heat until tender, approximately 5 minutes. Add a little rice wine or water if it begins to dry out. Add garlic and pepper and stir fry for 1 minute.

Add the scallions, sugar snap pease, pak choi and tofu, and stir fry for 2-3 minutes.

Add hoisin, soy sauce and cashew nuts and stir for 1 minute.

Serve piping hot onto plates – if you wish, you could add some toasted sesame seeds.

Nutritional Analysis	Per portion
Energy	358 kcal
Protein	25g
Carbohydrates	13g
Total Fat	23g
of which saturates	3g
Salt	3g
Sugar	8g
Fibre	8g

Traditional Tabbouleh

Tabbouleh is a classic Middle Eastern dish, eaten on all occasions and served as an accompaniment, or a full meal with grilled chicken or fish. There are various ways of making this dish, and you can combine other ingredients with it, if you prefer. The copious amounts of herbs bring this dish to life.

Serves: 4

Preparation Time: 15 minutes

Cook Time: 15-20 minutes for the freekeh

Ingredients:

- 9oz/250g freekeh, cooked
- 10 cherry tomatoes, halved or quartered
- 2 medium red onions <u>or</u> small bunch spring onions
- 1oz/25g fresh parsley, finely chopped
- 1oz/25g fresh coriander, finely chopped
- 1oz/25g fresh mint, finely chopped
- 2 cloves garlic, crushed

- 3tbsp olive oil
- 2tbsp lemon juice
- Grated zest of 1 lemon
- Salt and freshly ground black pepper to taste

Method:

Cook the freekeh as per packet instructions, rinse and leave to cool.

Prepare all the salad items and place in a medium sized bowl. Add the freekeh. Whisk together the lemon juice, zest, olive oil and garlic. Pour the dressing over the salad, add the seasoning and mix thoroughly together.

Serve on a decorative platter for a lunch, barbecue or dinner on a hot summer evening.

Nutritional Analysis	Per portion
Energy	320 kcal
Protein	5g
Carbohydrates	31g
of which sugars	4g
Total Fat	15g
of which saturates	3g
Fibre	5g

Turkey Stuffed "Beefsteak" Tomatoes

Turkey is very rich in high quality protein and low in fat, especially the white meat without the skin. It is also a good source of vitamins including folic acid that support immune and nerve function. This favorite in low-fat diets, is a key ingredient in this wonderful 'winter warmer' – and a way to get children eating vegetables.

Serves: 4

Preparation Time: 10 minutes

Cook Time: 25 minutes

Ingredients:

- 4 large beefsteak tomatoes
- 8oz/225g lean minced turkey
- 4oz/115g cooked freekeh
- 2tbsp/15g whole grain breadcrumbs
- Small handful fresh sage leaves, finely chopped
- 1 white onion, finely diced
- ½tsp ground black pepper
- 2 sticks of celery, finely diced
- 2tsp olive oil
- Salt to taste
- 1tsp ground cumin to taste (optional)

Method:

Heat oven to 160°C/325°F/Gas Mark 3. Heat the olive oil in a non-stick pan and sauté the onion and celery over low heat until softened, stirring to prevent burning. When softened, put the ground turkey mince and sage into the same pan and mix well until the turkey is slightly browned. Add the freekeh, cumin and breadcrumbs and mix well. Leave on a low heat, stirring well until the turkey is cooked through. Season with pepper, add salt or substitute to taste, if desired. Taste the mix, and if you want it a little spicier, add curry powder or cumin to heat it up a little. Leave to cool.

On a cutting board, take the tomatoes and cut off the stalk tops about 1 inch / 2cm down. Set aside, do not discard.

With a sharp knife, remove the inside core and flesh, being careful not to cut through the side of the tomato. On a clean, dry board, place some kitchen paper and turn the tomatoes upside down to drain out the seeds and excess moisture. Carve a little piece of the skin off the bottoms, so that the tomatoes will stand up while being cooked.

When drained, turn back over and fill the tomatoes with the turkey mix. Place in a deep baking dish in the oven and cook for 15 minutes. Take the tomatoes out and place the little tops back on. Place back in the oven and cook for an additional 20 minutes, or until they are soft to the touch.

Nutritional Analysis	Per Tomato
Energy	207kcal
Protein	23g
Carbohydrates	22g
of which sugars	4g
Total Fat	7g
of which saturates	1g
Fibre	5g
Sodium	.1g

Turkey Freekeh Meatball and Pineapple Curry

A delicious mild and coconut curry, with a hint of sweetness from pineapple and a little spice from the mango chutney.

Serves: 4

Preparation Time: 15 minutes

Cook Time: 20-25 minutes

Ingredients:

- 1lb/450g turkey mince
- 8oz/225g freekeh, cooked (half in the meatballs and half to serve extra)
- 1 onion, roughly chopped
- Very small piece of ginger, peeled and roughly chopped
- Small bunch coriander, roughly chopped
- 1lb/450g can pineapple chunks in juice, drained (reserve the juice)
- 1 heaped tbsp mango chutney
- 4tbsp Korma paste (or gluten-free alternative)
- 6tbsp ground almonds
- 1 garlic clove
- 1tbsp vegetable or sunflower oil

- 14fl.oz/400ml can low-fat coconut milk
- Naan bread (or gluten-free alternative), to serve

Method:

Season the turkey mince, add the freekeh and mango chutney, and shape into mini meatballs, about the size of a small tomato. Heat the oil in your widest pan, add the meatballs and cook, rolling them around the pan, for 8 mins until brown all over.

Meanwhile, in a food processor, blend the onion, ginger, garlic, coriander stalks and 2 tbsp of the reserved pineapple juice to a paste.

Push the meatballs to one side of the pan, tip the onion mixture into the space and cook for a few mins until softened.

Add the curry paste and stir for 1 min, coating the meatballs. Add the ground almonds, coconut milk, pineapple chunks, another 2 tbsp of the reserved pineapple juice and a little seasoning.

Simmer, uncovered, for 10 mins until thickened a little. Serve with extra freekeh, chopped coriander garnish and naan bread.

Nutritional Analysis	Per Tomato
Energy	456kcal
Protein	38g
Carbohydrates	18g
Fats	27g
Of which saturates	8g
Fibre	4g
Sodium	0.8g

SALADS

A Taste of the Islands Freekeh Salad

This is an interpretation of a salad served in Greece and its surrounding islands, and is absolutely delicious. The Greeks have been eating freekeh for years and years and were very surprised when asked what the grain was a few years ago! The salad comprises a lot of the wonderful ingredients you can find there, as well as our adaptation of the recipe.

Serves: 6-8

Preparation Time: 15 minutes

Cook Time: 15-20 minutes for the freekeh

Ingredients:

- 8oz/225g freekeh, cooked
- 7oz/200g green lentils, cooked, (can is easiest)
- 2tbsp almond slivers, lightly toasted
- 2tbsp pine nuts, lightly toasted
- 2 red onions, thinly sliced
- 1 bunch coriander, chopped
- Small bunch flat leaf parsley, chopped
- 4tbsp cornichons (gherkins) chopped
- Juice and grated rind of 1 lemon
- 3tbsp extra virgin olive oil
- Sea salt and ground black pepper to taste
- Juice and seeds of 2 pomegranates
- Large handful of sultanas
- 9oz/250g of thick yoghurt (preferably Greek)
- 1tsp fennel seeds
- 1 tbsp raw honey

Method:

Mix the yoghurt, honey and fennel seeds together in a bowl and leave to one side.

Place the fresh herbs, onion, freekeh, lentils, nuts, cornichons, sultanas, lemon and oil in a large bowl, mix thoroughly together.

Portion into dishes, or serve in one large dish, topped with the yoghurt dressing and the pomegranate.

Nutritional Analysis	Per portion
Energy	450kcal
Protein	16g
Carbohydrates	45g
of which sugars	7g
Total Fat	20g
of which saturates	2g
Fibre	9g
Sodium	.04g

Avocado Freekeh Salad with Sumac

The nutty but creamy flavour of a good ripe avocado is a perfect match with freekeh, and combines well with a strong flavoured dressing, with a hint of spice. Sumac has become a store cupboard essential, having a spicy smokey flavour which is wonderful when used in a dressing.

Serves: 6-8 as part of a meal or 3-4 as a lunch or brunch

Preparation Time: 10 minutes

Cook Time: 15-20 minutes for the freekeh

Ingredients:

- 7oz/200g freekeh, cooked
- 2 large avocados, skin and stone removed, and chopped into dice
- 1 red or green chilli, finely chopped (depends how hot you want it)
- 2 spring onions (scallions) chopped
- ½ small cucumber, cut into dice
- 4 large tomatoes, cut into dice
- 4tbsp fresh coriander, chopped

For the dressing

- 2tbsp balsamic vinegar
- 2 Dijon mustard
- 2tsp sumac
- 2tbsp olive oil
- 1tbsp agave nectar, grape molasses or raw honey
- Seasoning to taste

Method:

In a large bowl, mix together all the salad ingredients. Whisk the dressing ingredients thoroughly and pour over the salad.

Mix the cooled freekeh in with the salad and add any seasoning you require. Place on a plate, decorate with some chopped almonds or pine nuts and some lime wedges.

Nutritional Analysis	Per 1/8th
Energy	154kcal
Protein	5g
Carbohydrates	19
of which sugars	3g
Total Fat	7g
of which saturates	1g
Fibre	4g
Sodium	.1g

Freekeh Feta Greek Salad

A delicious Greek style salad, but incorporating healthy freekeh, which also makes the salad more filling. You can use any size of tomatoes or type of tomatoes, the choice is up to you.

Serves: 4

Preparation Time: 15 minutes (for the salad, 20 minutes plus cooling time for the freekeh)

Cook Time: 15-20 minutes for the freekeh (cook in advance if possible)

Ingredients:

- 7oz/200g freekeh, cooked
- 5 medium sized tomatoes, quartered
- ½ large cucumber, diced
- 2 medium sized red onions, finely sliced
- 2tbsp extra virgin olive oil
- Juice of 1 lemon
- 2tbsp fresh parsley, finely chopped
- 12 olives, chopped
- 5oz/140g feta cheese, crumbled
- Salt and freshly milled black pepper to taste

Method:

Try to cook the freekeh in advance and leave to cool covered in the fridge.

Make the dressing by combining the olive oil, lemon juice and parsley in a bowl and set aside.

Prepare the salad items as described, and mix together in a large bowl. Mix in the freekeh, and add the dressing. Combine everything together thoroughly, and season to taste. Add the crumbled feta.

Serve on a platter or in separate bowls with some sour dough bread.

Nutritional Analysis	Per Portion
Energy	596kcal
Protein	16g
Carbohydrates	40g
of which sugars	10g
Total Fat	10g
of which saturates	5g
Fibre	7g
Sodium	.5g

Simple Freekeh Buffet Salad

This salad is a very good accompaniment to buffet parties at home, or barbecues in the summer. Easy to make, filling and wholesome. Vary any dressings you want to make to give it a zing or a touch of sweetness, whichever you prefer. The celeriac is a lovely light 'mustardy' taste to add to this salad.

Serves: 6-8

Preparation Time: 15 minutes

Cook Time: 15-20 minutes for the freekeh

Ingredients:

- 1lb/450g freekeh
- 5oz/140g celeriac, finely shredded
- 5oz/140g red or white onion, finely chopped
- Large handful fresh parsley, finely chopped
- 20 cherry tomatoes, finely chopped
- Juice and grated rind of 1 lemon
- 2 lemons, quartered to garnish
- 34fl.oz/1 litre tomato juice
- 17fl.oz/½ litre water
- 2 cloves garlic, crushed
- 1tbsp olive oil
- Seasoning to taste

Method:

Mix the tomato juice and water together in a saucepan, and put the freekeh in to cook for 15-20 minutes until tender but with a slight bite.

Gently sauté the onion, garlic and celeriac with the olive oil in a large pan until soft. Leave to cool.

When cool, mix the cooked freekeh, and celeriac mix together in a large bowl. Add the finely chopped parsley, tomatoes, lemon juice and rind and stir to combine. Season to taste and serve garnished with the lemon quarters.

Nutritional Analysis	Per portion (1/6)
Energy	332kcal
Protein	20g
Carbohydrates	80g
of which sugars	4g
Total Fat	6g
of which saturates	1g
Fibre	13g
Sodium	.05g

Tuna Freekeh Provencale

A traditional Tuna Provencale salad incorporating freekeh as opposed to sliced potatoes which are the usual ingredient in France. You can use either fresh tuna lightly seared, or cans of tuna, preferably in spring water (not in brine or oil) to avoid more fats or salt. Olive oil is part of the dressing, so less oil or salt in the can would be preferable.

Serves: 4

Preparation Time: 15 – 20 minutes

Cook Time: 6 minutes (for the eggs)

Ingredients:

- 7oz/200g freekeh, cooked
- 2 eggs, hardboiled
- 1 x 14oz/400g tuna, drained
- 4 large tomatoes, quartered
- 2 red onions, finely sliced
- ½ large cucumber, diced
- ½ crisp lettuce such as Little Gem or Cos, roughly chopped
- 2tbsp capers, chopped
- 2 handfuls of Provence black olives, halved
- 2tbsp olive oil
- 1tbsp white wine vinegar
- 1tsp Dijon mustard
- Salt and pepper to taste
- 2 stems of fresh basil, leaves removed and finely sliced

Nutritional Analysis	Per Portion
Energy	393kcal
Protein	59g
Carbohydrates	37g
of which sugars	6.5g
Total Fat	15g
of which saturates	6g
Fibre	7g
Sodium	.8g

Zingy Thai Chicken and Mango Freekeh Salad

Asian flavours such as lime and light soy sauce bring this salad to life and to keep it authentic. We have used pak choi (bok choi) as the 'leafy' part of this dish. Depending how hot you enjoy your food, use mild chillies to make it more 'user friendly'! Mango always pairs wonderfully with chicken, and the dressing gives it a lovely 'zing'. A great summer dish for outdoor entertaining.

Serves: 6

Preparation Time: 10-15 minutes

Cook Time: 15-20 minutes (for the freekeh)

Ingredients:

- 7oz/200g freekeh, cooked
- 5 large skinless and boneless chicken breasts
- 2 pak choi, roughly chopped
- 1 cucumber, peeled and diced
- 6 fresh baby corn, sliced lengthways through the middle
- Large handful mange tout, any stalks removed
- 2 medium sized carrots, peeled and julienned (cut into thin matchsticks)
- 6 radishes or daikon, thinly sliced
- 1 large or 2 medium sized mangoes, peeled, stone removed and diced
- 1 small red or green chilli, finely chopped
- Handful of unsalted peanuts, crushed
- 1 small red onion or 2 or 3 scallions, thinly sliced

For the dressing

- 3tbsp sesame oil
- 1½tbsp light soy sauce
- Juice of 2 limes, zest of 1 lime
- 2 cloves garlic, finely chopped

Method:

Heat oven to 180°C/350°F/Gas mark 4

In a large baking dish, place the chicken breasts and top up with water so that the breasts are completely covered.

Poach the chicken in the oven for 35-40 minutes until cooked through. Drain off all the water, remove the chicken breasts and leave to cool on a cold plate.

Mix all of the dressing ingredients together and set aside. In a large bowl, mix all of the salad ingredients together with the freekeh and mangoes. Shred or thinly slice the chicken when cold enough, and put into the salad.

Pour over the dressing and toss everything together.

This dish looks stunning served on a big platter topped with the crushed peanuts and red onion for everyone to help themselves. Decorate with lime quarters if you have any.

Nutritional Analysis	Per Portion
Energy	361kcal
Protein	34g
Carbohydrates	26g
of which sugars	6g
Total Fat	15g
of which saturates	3g
Fibre	6g
Sodium	.3g

SNACKS

Freekeh Chocolate Biscuit Cakes

A little like chocolate rice cakes but using low fat biscuits that are crumbled into the mixture with the freekeh. The children will really like these and no need to tell them if you don't want to, that there is freekeh in there!

Serves: 12 small cakes

Preparation Time: 5 minutes

Cook Time: 25 minutes (including freekeh)

Ingredients:

- 3½oz/100g freekeh, cooked
- 5oz/140g chocolate
- 5oz/140g unsalted butter
- 2tbsp runny honey
- 3tbsp mixed dried chopped fruit
- 5 or 6 low fat biscuits, crushed with a rolling pin

Method:

Over a very low heat, melt the chocolate and butter. Add the honey and stir frequently until melted and combined.

Put the cooked freekeh, crushed biscuits and dried fruit into the mix and stir until combined.

Spoon the mix into small cake cases and leave to set. If you want the cakes to be really chocolatey, add mini chocolate eggs on top before setting.

Nutritional Analysis	Per Cake
Energy	243kcal
Protein	11g
Carbohydrates	24g
of which sugars	15g
Total Fat	12g
of which saturates	9g
Fibre	6g
Sodium	.1g

Freekeh Meatless Meatballs (Felafels)

This recipe can be used for either 'meatballs' or the delicious felafels served in the Middle East as very much part of a buffet or mezze. Serve as a main course with mashed sweet potatoes, or with a garlic dip or tzatsiki dip with fresh mint, for a starter or buffet.

Serves: 24 meatballs

Preparation Time: 20 minutes

Cook Time: 20 minutes

Ingredients:

- 6oz/170g freekeh, cooked
- 1 sweet potato, grated
- 2 garlic cloves, crushed or minced
- 2tbsp coriander, finely chopped
- 4oz/115g brown breadcrumbs
- 2 eggs, beaten
- Freshly ground black pepper
- 2tsp ground cumin
- Salt to taste
- Olive oil for brushing (approx 1½ tbsp)
- 2tbsp currants (optional)

Method

Heat oven to 180°C/350°F/Gas mark 4.

Line 2 baking sheets with parchment paper, and lightly brush with the oil.

Add all the ingredients together in a large bowl, mix well to combine.

Make the 'meatballs' by dividing the mixture into approximately 1 ½ heaped tablespoons and gently rolling into a ball, or an oblong shape, in the palms of your hands.

Place the balls onto the baking sheets and cook for 15 minutes, or until golden brown on the top. Turn over and cook for a further 5 minutes. (The tray on the second shelf may need a little longer).

Serve as an appetiser or as a main course.

Nutritional Analysis	Per 6 Balls
Energy	212kcal
Protein	8g
Carbohydrates	37g
of which sugars	9g
Total Fat	7g
of which saturates	6g
Fibre	6g
Sodium	.2g

Freekeh Sausage and Red Pepper Rolls

A twist on a traditional sausage roll, these are lovely herby sausage rolls with chopped red pepper and using tortilla wraps as the 'pastry', cutting down on the fat content of the dish, but certainly not detracting from the flavour. As a vegetarian option, you could try freekeh mixed with cheese, onion and herbs, equally as delicious.

Serves: 16 medium sized rolls, or 12 larger ones

Preparation Time: 20 minutes

Cook Time: 25-30 minutes

Ingredients:

- 1lb/450g good quality sausage meat
- 5oz/140g freekeh, cooked
- 1 large red pepper, finely diced
- 1 onion, finely diced
- 2tsps dried mixed herbs
- 4 tortilla wraps
- Oil for sealing the wraps

Method:

Heat oven to 180°C/350°F/Gas mark 4 and line a baking tray with foil.

Mix the sausage meat, cooked freekeh, onion, red pepper and herbs together in a bowl.

Lay out 4 tortillas and starting on one side, lay out the sausage meat in a long sausage shape, leaving about 3cm/1inch on each side. Roll the wrap up over the sausage meat and tuck in the edges as you go.

Just before the end, brush with oil to seal, and then brush over the outside of the wrap with a little more oil.

Bake in the oven for 25-30 minutes until crisp and golden brown. Leave to cool, then cut into 3 or 4 pieces to form the smaller sausage rolls.

Nutritional Analysis	Per Portion
Energy	290kcal
Protein	7g
Carbohydrates	25g
of which sugars	0g
Total Fat	22g
of which saturates	10g
Fibre	3g
Sodium	1.8g

Rustic Freekeh Bruschettas

Italian bruschettas are a great snack to make quickly and you can use tomatoes that are beginning to go soft, and French bread or ciabattas that may be going a little stale! Whichever way, these are delicious either as a quick snack, or as part of a buffet for guests.

Serves: 4

Preparation Time: 15 minutes (including grilling bread)

Cook Time: Included in preparation time

Ingredients:

- 8 slices of French bread or ciabatta, cut diagonally
- 6oz/170g freekeh, cooked
- 3 large tomatoes, finely chopped or diced
- 1 medium sized onion, very finely diced
- 1 clove garlic, skinned and cut in half for 'rubbing'
- 2 garlic cloves, very finely chopped
- 10 fresh basil leaves, shredded
- 3 slices Parma ham, torn into strips

- Olive oil to dress
- Freshly ground black pepper to season

Method:

Lightly grill or pan fry the bread in a griddle pan. When lightly brown, cool and rub with the garlic clove and set aside.

In a large bowl, mix together the freekeh, chopped tomatoes, onions and garlic.

Heap the mix onto the slices of bread, top with the shredded basil, Parma ham and ground black pepper and drizzle with olive oil.

Nutritional Analysis	Per Portion
Energy	225kcal
Protein	11g
Carbohydrates	35g
of which sugars	4g
Total Fat	6g
of which saturates	6g
Fibre	5g
Sodium	.3g

Zucchini and Freekeh Fritters

So simple to make and a great way of using up left over freekeh. You could also make these fritters as carrot and coriander with freekeh for a different taste, or even sweetcorn. We have used mint to bring out the flavour of the courgettes, but you can use another herb if you want to, such as oregano.

Serves: 2-3

Preparation Time: 10-15 minutes

Cook Time: 10 minutes

Ingredients:

- 4oz/115g freekeh, cooked
- 1 large or 2 medium sized courgettes, grated
- 1 small onion, grated
- 2 cloves garlic, crushed
- 2oz/55g parmesan cheese, grated
- 2 heaped tbsp plain flour
- 1tbsp fresh mint, finely chopped
- 1tbsp olive oil
- Freshly ground black pepper

Method:

If you can, squeeze some moisture from both the grated courgettes and onion, so they are not too wet.

Mix together all the ingredients, apart from the olive oil. Form into balls in the palm of your hand (about the size of a golf ball) and then gently flatten.

Heat a frying pan with the oil and place each fritter into the pan, so that they are not touching. You can fry them in two batches, keeping the first batch warm.

Fry each side for 4-5 minutes until golden brown

Serve with a roasted pepper dip/sauce and a little salad.

Nutritional Analysis	Per Portion
Energy	177 Kcals
Protein	9g
Carbohydrates	14g
Of which sugars	2g
Total Fat	9g
of which saturates	3g
Fibre	2g

California Sushi Roll with Pickled Ginger

As bad as it is to say it, you really do have to have the right equipment for making any form of sushi – bamboo mat in particular! We have changed the sticky sushi rice to freekeh, so rolling with a mat is vital as the freekeh consistency does differ quite a lot to sticky rice. We have made it 'sticky' by adding some sweet chilli sauce – it does work! California sushi rolls are made with crab sticks, or imitation crab which makes it a little easier to roll and form a nice looking piece of sushi.

Serves: 4 as a snack

Preparation Time: 30-40 minutes (until you get used to it!)

Cook Time: Use ready cooked freekeh

Ingredients:

- 3-4oz/85-115g of freekeh, cooked
- 1 nori (seaweed) sheet
- 3oz/85g crab sticks
- 1 ripe avocado, sliced
- 2oz/55g white sesame seeds (or black if you prefer)
- 1tbsp pickled ginger
- 2tbsp sweet chilli sauce
- Shrimp to accompany each sushi piece

To serve:

- Extra sweet chilli sauce, soy sauce and wasabi

Method:

Mix the cooked freekeh with a little chilli sauce at a time, until you get a sticky consistency. Set aside.

Break the nori sheet in half and cover the mat with cling film. Place one half on the mat, shiny side face down.

Take a handful of the freekeh mix and spread over the nori, approximately ½ inch/1 cm high. Sprinkle a little light soy sauce over the freekeh and top with a layer of sesame seeds.

Flip the nori over, so that the rice is now facing downwards. Line the crabsticks up along the freekeh and nori, and the slices of avocado next to them (1 or 2 slices).

Roll up the nori, pulling the cling film away as you roll, and when tight, cut into 8 pieces.

Place on a decorative plate, intersperse with medium sized shrimp. Top the shrimp with a little pickled ginger and a small drop of sweet chilli.

Repeat the process until you have enough snacks for your guests!

You can make this with tuna, prawns or other fish depending on your taste. Try also using cucumber with or as an alternative to avocado.

Serve with additional sweet chilli sauce, soy sauce and wasabi.

Nutritional Analysis	Per roll
Energy	186kcals
Protein	4g
Carbohydrates	7g
of which sugars	0.5g
Total Fat	2.0g
of which saturates	0.3g
Sodium	0.24g

INDEX

7oz, 38
agave nectar, 35
agave syrup, 20, 45, 47, 97
allergens, 8
allspice, 70
almond, 131
almond milk, 29
almonds, 12, 18, 23, 71, 126
AMARANTH, 14
apple, 21
Apple, 106
Apple Crumble, 49
apple juice, 107
apples, 50
applesauce, 18
Apricot, 45
apricots, 26, 29, 45
aubergine, 79
avocado, 161
Avocado, 133
avocados, 134
baby asparagus spears, 97
baby corn, 144
baby spinach, 68, 82, 113
bacon, 88
baked bread, 14
baking powder, 38, 40
baking soda, 17, 38, 41
balsamic vinegar, 104
balti curry paste, 68
bamboo mat, 160
banana chips, 18
Banana Freekeh Kisses, 47

bananas, 21, 47
basil, 34, 35, 53, 92, 142, 155
beef, 113
Beef, 112
beef stock, 61
beef stock cube, 65
Beef Stroganoff, 61
Beefsteak Tomatoes, 123
beets, 104
berries, 34
biscuits, 147
black bean, 12
black olives, 92, 142
black onion seeds, 41
black pepper, 82, 92
blackberries, 50
Blackberry, 49
blueberries, 23, 29
borlotti beans, 12
bowel movements, 7
breadcrumbs, 82, 149
breadmaking, 15
Breakfast and Morning
   Coffee Time, 16
broad beans, 13
broccoli, 118
broth, 57
Brown Rice, 6
Brown rice flour, 110
brown rice syrup, 45
brown sugar, 17, 26, 41
Bruschettas, 155
buffalo mozzarella, 52

Buffet Salad, 138
bulgur wheat', 5
butter, 23, 32
button, 70
button mushrooms, 61
cabbage, 13
Cajun seasoning, 74
Cajun Seasoning, 76
Cakes and Loaves, 36
calcium, 8
Calcium, 6
California Sushi Roll with Pickled Ginger, 160
California sushi rolls, 160
Calories, 6
can chopped tomatoes, 76
canned lentils, 12
canola, 18
canola oil, 26, 115
capers, 142
carbohydrate, 13
carbohydrates, 7
Carbs, 6
cardamom, 45
carrot, 110, 157
Carrot, 17
carrots, 17, 38, 100, 107, 144
cashew nuts, 118
caster sugar, 50
celeriac, 139
celery, 57, 76, 88, 107, 113, 124
cheddar cheese, 79
cheese, 15, 52
cherries, 23
cherry tomatoes, 33, 52, 92, 121, 139
chestnut, 70
Chia, 12
CHIA, 14
chicken, 85, 115, 144
chicken stock cubes, 76, 101
chickpeas, 12, 110
child friendly recipes, 13
chilli, 14, 42, 134
Chilli Con Carne, 64
chilli powder, 65, 76, 100, 110
chilli sauce, 161
chips, 74
Chips, 73
chives, 32, 82
chocolate, 14, 147
Chocolate Biscuit Cakes, 147
chopped tomatoes, 65
ciabatta, 155
cinnamon, 8, 14, 17, 23, 29, 45, 50, 55, 86
citrus, 14
Coconut, 17
coconut curry, 126
coconut milk, 45, 127
Coffee, 37
coffee essence, 38
Cookies, 26
cooking apples, 107
coriander, 8, 12, 57, 68, 88, 94, 110, 121, 126, 131, 134, 149, 157
cornichons, 131
Cos, 142
courgette, 110
courgettes, 157, 158
crab, 160
crab sticks, 160, 161

Cracked Freekeh, 9
cracked freekeh', 4
cranberries, 23, 26, 86
crème fraiche, 62, 79
cucumber, 68, 71, 134, 136, 142, 144
cumin, 8, 57, 65, 124, 149
cured meats, 14
currants, 149
curry, 12
daikon, 144
Demerara sugar, 50
Dessert, 45
Desserts and Snacks, 44
dessicated coconut, 47
Dijon mustard, 61, 142
Dinners, 60
dressings, 14
dried berries, 23
dried chopped fruit, 147
dried coconut, 17
Dried fruit, 14
dried mixed herbs, 153
eggs, 17, 26, 38, 41, 88, 142, 149
Egypt, 5
extra virgin olive oil, 131, 136
fajita seasoning, 94
farik, 3
farikiyya, 5
farro, 14
Farro, 6
FARRO, 14
Fat, 6
fennel seeds, 131
feta cheese, 92, 136
Feta Greek Salad, 136

fibre, 7
Fibre, 6
field, 70
figs, 55
Figs, 54
flageolet beans, 12
Flapjacks, 20
flatbreads, 94
France, 141
freekah, 3
freekeh, 3, 4, 13
Freekeh, 6, 13
Freekeh Potato Cakes, 31
freeze, 11
French bread, 155
French toast, 42
frikeh, 3
fritters, 11
Fritters, 157
garam massala, 57
garlic, 65, 76, 79, 86, 88, 94, 110, 113, 115, 118, 121, 126, 139, 155, 158
garlic cloves, 71, 149
garlic dip, 149
garlic flatbread, 94
gherkins, 131
ginger, 126, 161
Gluten, 8
gluten-free, 126, 127
goats cheese, 104
goji berries, 17
Goji Berry Muffins, 17
good chicken, 107
grains, 13
Granola Bars, 23
Greece, 5, 130

Greek yoghurt, 71, 104
Greek Yoghurt, 35
green, 4, 134
green beans, 13
green chilli, 144
green lentils, 131
green pepper, 76, 79, 115
ground beef, 88
ground cinnamon, 41
ground nutmeg, 82
guacamole, 94
ham, 52, 53
hazelnuts, 15, 26
Health, 6
Herb Crusted Salmon, 82
Herb Pilaff, 70
herbs, 14, 15
hoisin sauce, 118
honey, 14, 41, 55, 104, 147
IBS, 7
Iraq, 5
iron, 8
Iron, 6
Italian foods, 14
Jordan, 5
kale, 13, 57
KAMUT, 14
kidney beans, 12
Kids, 52
Korma, 126
lamb, 68
Lamb Biryani, 67
lamb stock, 68
laxation, 7
leafy green vegetables, 13
Lebanon, 5
leek, 57
lemon, 82, 110, 122, 131, 136, 139
lemon juice, 70
Lentil Casserole, 106
light soy sauce, 118
lime, 34, 35
Little Gem, 142
Little Ones, 73
Loaf, 40
lutein, 8
macular degeneration, 8
mange tout, 116, 144
mango, 34
Mango, 143
mango chutney, 126
mangoes, 34, 144
maple, 20, 97
Maple Roasted Chicken, 85
maple syrup, 29, 85
mashed potato, 31
meatballs, 126
Meatless Meatballs (Felafels), 149
Meatloaf, 88
Mediterranean, 14, 91
Mediterranean foods, 15
melons, 34
Mexican Beef, 94
Middle East, 5
Middle Eastern, 11, 14
milk, 38
minced, 88
minced beef, 65, 94
minced pork, 74
minced turkey, 124
mint, 8, 34, 55, 62, 68, 71, 121, 158

Mint, 12
Minted Pea, 61
miso, 12
mixed spice, 18, 38
molasses, 41
muscovado sugar, 23, 115
Mushroom, 70
mushrooms, 70, 79, 113
mustard, 85, 110, 113
mustard seeds, 41, 110
Naan bread, 127
nori, 161
North Africa, 5
nutmeg, 8, 41, 50
nutrients, 15
Nutrition, 6
nuts, 14
Nuts, 12
oats, 20
olive oil, 41, 57, 61, 79, 85, 92, 101, 104, 124, 139, 142, 158
Olive oil, 149, 156
olives, 136
Olives, 112
onion, 31, 57, 65, 68, 74, 86, 94, 97, 110, 113, 115, 124, 126, 139, 144, 153, 155, 158
onions, 70, 76, 88, 100, 107, 121, 131, 142
orange, 18, 85
oregano, 12, 157
orzo, 11
oyster sauce, 12
paella, 76
pak choi, 118, 144
pancetta, 55, 88
papayas, 34

paprika, 8, 14, 65
Parma ham, 55, 155
parmesan, 14
parmesan cheese, 158
parsley, 12, 71, 79, 82, 86, 88, 121, 131, 136, 139
parsnips, 13, 97, 107
pasta, 11
pea, 13
peanut butter, 21
peas, 62
pecans, 18
pepper, 118
peppers, 13
pilaff, 12, 14
pilaffs, 8
pine nuts, 12, 47, 55, 71, 92, 113, 131
pineapple, 34, 52, 126
Pineapple Curry, 126
pineapple pieces, 116
pistachios, 12, 29, 45
pitta bread, 52
pitta breads, 52
Pizza, 94
Pizza Margharita, 52
plain flour, 158
pomegranate, 12
pomegranates, 131
pork, 107
Pork, 106
porridge, 14
Porridge, 29
potatoes, 13, 74
pregnant, 8
pressure cooker, 10
Protein, 6

Provencale, 141
pumpkin, 100
pumpkin puree, 41
pumpkin seeds, 41
puy lentils, 107
quinoa, 15
Quinoa, 6, 14
QUINOA, 14
radishes, 144
raisins, 26
Raita, 68
rapeseed oil, 110
Ras-al-Hanout, 8
raspberries, 29
raw honey, 20, 23, 26, 29, 35, 47, 131
red, 76, 79, 92, 115, 134, 144
red kidney beans, 65
red onion, 61
red pepper, 74, 153
Red Pepper Rolls, 152
red peppers, 100
red pesto, 52
rice, 11, 160
rice cooker, 9
Rice Cooker –, 10
Ricotta, 54
ricotta cheese, 55
risottos, 14
roasted, 14
Roasted Balsamic Beets, 103
roasted peppers, 11
Roasted Root Vegetables, 97
Roasted Vegetable, 100
Rocket, 104
rolled oats, 21, 23, 26
rosemary, 8, 12, 79

rubbing, 4
rump steak, 61
Rustic, 155
sage, 124
Salad, 130, 143
salads, 8, 11, 14
Salads, 129
salmon fillets, 82
Sausage, 73, 152
sausage meat, 153
scallion, 77
scallions, 118, 134, 144
Scrambled Eggs, 31
seaweed, 161
seeds, 12
Sesame, 12
sesame seeds, 23
shallots, 61
shitake, 70
shrimp, 76
Shrimp, 161
Shrimp Gumbo, 76
single cream, 32, 79
slow cookers/crockpots, 10
smoked salmon, 32
Smoked Salmon, 31
smoothies, 14
Snacks, 146
Soup, 100
soups, 8, 11, 14
sour cream, 62
Sour cream, 94
soy sauce, 161
spelt, 11
SPELT, 15
Spiced Pumpkin, 40
Spicy, 109

spinach, 13
Spinach, 82
spring onions, 121, 134
starch, 11
steak, 94
stews, 8, 14
stir frys, 11
stock, 12
strawberries, 34
Stuffed Peppers, 91
stuffing, 85
Stuffing, 85
stuffings, 14, 15
sugar, 38, 65
sugar snap peas, 116, 118
sultanas, 26, 68, 131
sumac, 101
Sumac, 8, 133
sundried tomatoes, 11, 79
sunflower oil, 107, 126
sunflower seeds, 23
Supergrains, 3
sushi, 160, 161
sushi rice, 160
swede, 13, 97
Sweet and Sour Chicken, 115
sweet chilli sauce, 12, 160, 161
sweet potato, 149
sweet potatoes, 13, 57, 97, 149
sweetcorn, 76, 157
Syria, 5
Tabbouleh, 121
taco, 94
Taste of the Islands, 130
TEFF, 15
thyme, 79, 104

tinned tomatoes, 11
tofu, 118
Tofu, 118
tomato, 52
tomato juice, 139
tomato ketchup, 115
tomato puree, 11, 52, 62, 65, 94
tomatoes, 100, 134, 136, 142, 155
tortilla wraps, 153
tuna, 142
Tuna, 141
Turkey, 5, 123, 126
Turkey Freekeh Meatball, 126
turkey mince, 126
tzatsiki, 149
unsalted butter, 147
unsalted peanuts, 144
vanilla extract, 18, 26, 45
veganism, 4
vegetable, 126
Vegetable Bake, 79
vegetable oil, 18, 26, 38, 115
Vegetable Stew, 57
Vegetable Stir Fry, 118
vegetable stock, 57, 70, 107
vegetables, 14
vegetarianism, 4
Veggie Burgers, 109
Walnut Cake, 37
walnuts, 18, 23, 38
wasabi, 12, 161
watercress, 33
wheat, 4, 8
white sesame seeds, 161
white wine vinegar, 115, 142

whole grain breadcrumbs, 124
Wholegrain, 4
Wholegrain Freekeh, 9
wholemeal, 38
wholemeal flour, 17
with soy sauce, 12
yellow pepper, 92

yoghurt, 68, 131
Yoghurt, 103
zeaxanthin, 8
Zingy Thai Chicken, 143
ziplock bags, 11
zucchini, 13
Zucchini, 157

www.ingramcontent.com/pod-product-compliance
Lightning Source LLC
Chambersburg PA
CBHW070154100426
42743CB00013B/2901